# Quilling

## 20 Beautiful Designs

Sena Runa

# Contents

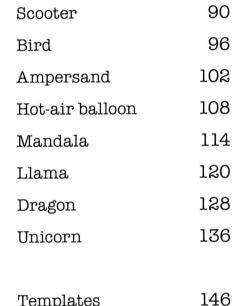

# Introduction

Quilling is a beautiful paper craft that involves forming works of art from strips of paper. It's a very old technique that had almost been forgotten, but with the help of talented artists and art lovers around the world, quilling is gaining in popularity once more.

I first discovered quilling in 2013. My intention had been to enjoy it as a hobby alongside my career, but I found quilling so satisfying that I soon decided I wanted to focus on it full time. Back then, there were very few people making quilled art, but in recent years it has boomed, and I have met many people who have been inspired by images of quilling that they have seen on the Internet and social media sites. These people have all wanted a good resource from which to learn the craft, and that is what I aimed to provide with my first book, *Quilling Art*, published in 2017. Since then, quilling has become even more popular, and I decided to write another book to satisfy the increasing demand for information and tutorials. So here it is, with 20 new and exciting projects to make.

The book starts with everything you need to know before you begin the projects. There are pages on the tools and materials you'll need, a section on all the techniques required, and useful information about measuring and placing shapes. All of the projects provide detailed instructions and clear step-by-step photographs that are easy to follow and understand. To help you create your works of art, you will also find actual-size templates at the back of the book for each project.

The projects cover a wide range of subjects and will appeal to people of all ages. They make fabulous cards and framed pictures to give as gifts, while some, such as the Rainbow and the Hot-air Balloon, look lovely hung with ribbon around the home. The projects get progressively more difficult, so if you're a beginner it's best to start at the beginning and work your way through. Once you have practised and gained confidence, you can go on to create your own unique works of art, experimenting with different colours and shapes.

I wrote this book to inspire new and existing quilling devotees and, in so doing, help to continue this wonderful art form. My hope is that people who discover the beautiful art of quilling through this book will then take it to the next level, creating their own unique quilling works of art.

**Sena Runa**

# Tools & materials

Quilling requires little more than paper, glue and scissors, but you'll get much better results by investing in a few additional tools. We've suggested the most useful ones in this book, but others are available.

## CUTTING MAT (A)

Any cutting mat is suitable for the projects in this book. A self-healing mat is ideal if you will be using it for a long period of time. It is also a good choice for making straight cuts that require applying a lot of pressure. Some mats come with marks that indicate angles of different sizes.

## RULER (B)

You will need a ruler to check the size of a paper strip and to measure for the correct length. It's also helpful for checking the size of other shapes that you prepare. If you cut your own paper strips at home, you should use a metal ruler – it will provide a firm edge for cutting against with a craft knife.

## CIRCULAR RULER (C)

When making coils, you can use a circular ruler (sometimes called a circle sizer) to check their sizes. Some are marked with the diameters of the circles. A circular ruler is really useful for making coils that are all the same size and for creating symmetrical shapes.

## QUILLING TOOL (D)

A special quilling tool has a slotted end for holding paper strips while making coils, but it is not essential if you prefer to use your fingers.

## QUILLING NEEDLE (E)

To trace a template outline onto the base paper, you will need a quilling needle or a similar tool, such as a compass. Choose one with a fine tip – but not one with a very sharp tip, which may damage the paper when tracing on it. The needle should be strong so that it doesn't bend under pressure as you press on the paper.

## TWEEZERS (F)

A fine-tipped pair of tweezers is useful for holding and placing shapes onto the outlines, especially when it comes to small projects. Look for tweezers that you find comfortable to hold and that are easy to use.

## SCISSORS (G)

For quilling, choose a medium-sized pair of scissors with fine-pointed ends; you will be using these for both cutting the paper and bending it. If you prefer, you can use bigger scissors for cutting the larger pieces of cardstock, but you will also need a smaller pair for detailed cutting.

## WHITE GLUE (H)

To glue the shapes to the base paper, the best choice is white craft paper glue, because it dries clear and will be invisible. A liquid glue is easier to apply, especially if you use it with a needle-nosed bottle. It's also a good idea to choose an easy-to-remove version that is easier to clean off both your tools and your hands.

## CRAFT KNIFE (I)

To make precise cuts, the best tool for cutting strips of paper and card is a craft knife. The blades are replaceable – always make sure you use a sharp blade for the best results.

## PAPER (J)

For quilling, you'll need two types of paper: 22–32lb (80–120gsm) coloured acid-free paper for the strips and 90lb (250gsm) cardstock for the base paper and outlines. Your projects will last longer with acid-free paper, because it keeps its colour much longer than other types, and you'll find that lighter or heavier papers than those suggested here are harder to roll and work for quilling.

Ready-made quilling sets are available that include pre-cut colourful strips. However you can cut your own strips at home using a craft knife. All the projects in this book use paper that is 1cm wide, but other sizes are available too (5mm, 3mm). You can use any colour you like for the projects – the ones used in this book are just suggestions. Cardstock will need to be cut at home using a craft knife.

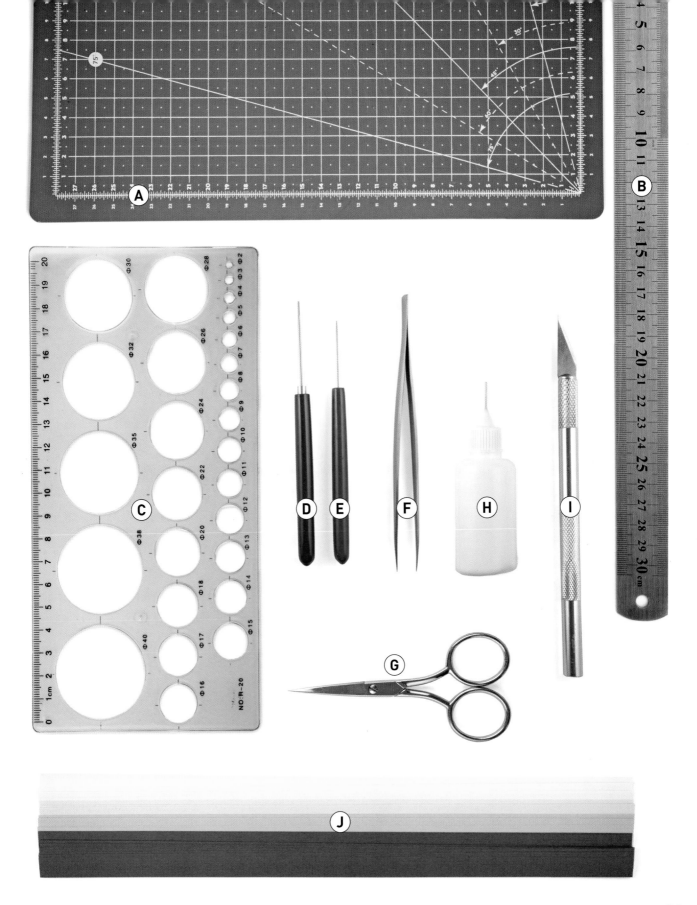

# Techniques

## Creating an outline

To create the projects in this book, you will need to make a cardstock outline copied from a template. When the outline is ready, you can then fill it with a variety of coiled and curved paper shapes. Follow the steps here, using a cloud shape as an example, as a guide for setting up an outline.

**1**

For the base, place the template over a blank sheet of 90lb (250gsm) cardstock. Use a quilling needle or compass to trace around the outside of the template and over the lines, then remove the template. You should be able to see the tracing on the base cardstock.

**2**

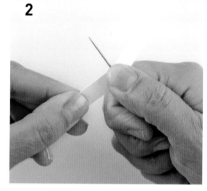

To make the edges of the outline, cut a ⅜in (1cm)-wide strip from a piece of 90lb (250gsm) cardstock. Bend the strip around the quilling needle to create a curve.

**3**

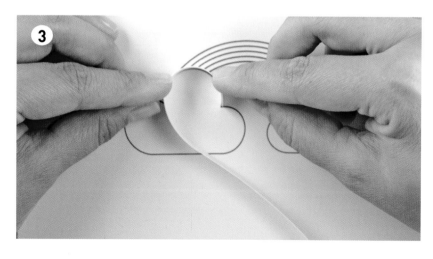

Place the cardstock strip on top of the template and shape it to fit in the curve where you are working in the outline.

**4**

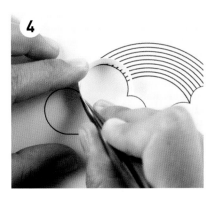

Now use a pair of tweezers to mark on the strip the point on the outline where it will fold.

**5**

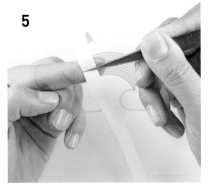

Fold the strip where you have made the mark with the tweezers – you can use the tweezers to help make a crisp edge.

**6**

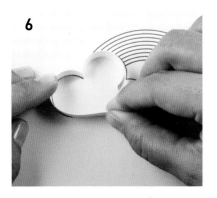

Continue to shape the remaining part of the shape in the same way, in this case until the strip ends where the cloud started.

**7**

After creating the curves, you should have a shape similar to the shape on your template. Check it against the tracing on the base to make sure that it fits well.

**8**

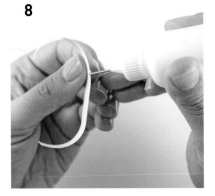

Apply a thin layer of glue along the edge of the strip that will touch the base cardstock. Make sure it's not too thick, or it may be visible when dry.

**9**

Place the cardstock strip over the traced outline, making sure that the ends of the strip align neatly.

**10**

Press gently so the cardstock strip stays in place. This part of the outline is complete. Continue until all the shapes copied from the template are complete.

# Creating shapes

In this section you'll learn how to make all the shapes used in this book, including coils, scrolls and waves. In case you prefer to use your fingers rather than a quilling tool, we've included both methods for making basic coils. You can use a circular ruler if you want to keep the sizes consistent.

## COIL – USING A QUILLING TOOL

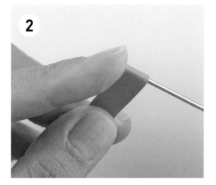

**1**

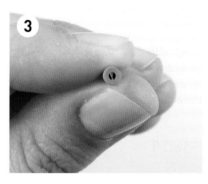

**2**

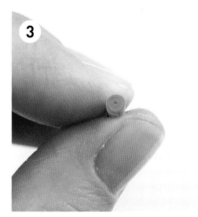

**3**

Place the edge of a strip of paper into the slot at the end of the quilling tool.

Twirl the quilling tool while you hold the end of the paper strip tightly with your other hand. To keep the coil straight, push the side of it gently as you twirl.

When you finish twirling the paper, you should have a coil that looks like the one shown here. Hold it tightly with one hand and pull the tool out.

## COIL – USING YOUR FINGERS

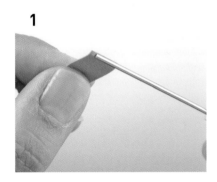

**1**

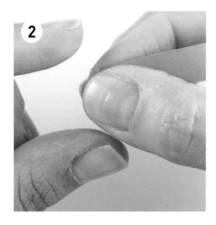

**2**

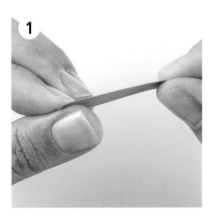

**3**

Begin by folding over the tip of the end of a paper strip, as shown here.

Now roll the strip using your thumb and index finger. Keep the coil straight by pushing gently on it from both sides with your other hand.

When you finish rolling the paper, you should have a coil that looks like the one shown here.

# WAYS TO FINISH A COIL

### BASIC COIL

After rolling a paper strip into a coil (see facing page), let it expand by loosening it slightly, then glue down the edge of the paper.

### OPEN COIL

After rolling a paper strip into a coil (see facing page), allow the end of the strip to loosen a little.

### TIGHT COIL

Make a coil (see facing page), then without letting it expand, apply a thin layer of glue to the end of the paper strip to tightly seal it.

### SEMI-TIGHT COIL

Make a tight coil (see above), but slightly loosen it to allow the centre to expand before applying the glue.

### TIGHT COIL COVERED WITH PAPER

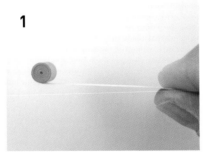

**1** Prepare a tight coil (see above). Apply a thin layer of glue to the end of a different-coloured paper strip and attach it to the tight coil.

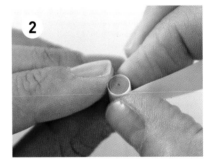

**2** Wrap the rest of the strip around the tight coil.

**3** Holding the coil with a pair of tweezers, apply a thin layer of glue to the end of the paper strip.

**4** Secure the end of the paper to the coil and leave to dry.

## C SCROLL

Roll a paper strip into a coil (see page 10). Loosen and unroll the coil a little, then roll the free end of the strip into another smaller coil.

## ASYMMETRIC SCROLL

Make an open coil (see page 11). Using a pen or straw, curve the end of the strip in the opposite direction to the coil.

## S SCROLL

Make an asymmetric scroll (see left), then roll the free end of the strip to make a smaller coil in the opposite direction to the top coil.

## S SHAPE

**1**

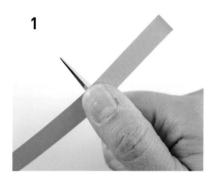

Starting about halfway along a paper strip and continuing to one end of the paper, run the edge of a pair of scissors along the strip.

**2**

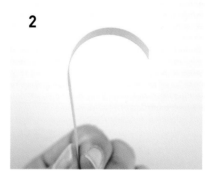

This will curve the paper strip to one side, creating the upper side of the S shape.

**3**

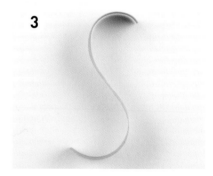

Repeat the process at the other end of the strip, but in the opposite direction to create the bottom of the S shape.

## C SHAPE

Run the edge of a pair of scissors all the way along one side of a paper strip to curve it into a C. To make a curve in a paper strip that has straight ends, similar to a U shape, start partway along the strip and finish before you get to the end.

## WAVE SHAPE

**1**

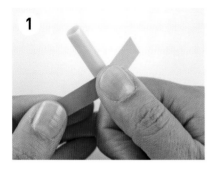

Starting near the end of a paper strip, use a pen or straw to make a gentle curve on one side of the strip.

**2**

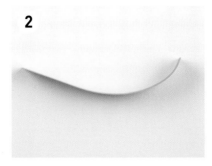

You should have a strip with a single gentle curve.

**3**

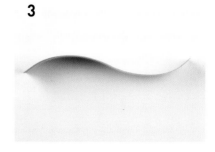

Now curve the other end of the strip in the opposite direction to make a wave shape with two similar curves.

## ASYMMETRIC WAVE SHAPE

This is similar to the wave shape (see above), but only slightly curve the second end in the opposite direction to create uneven curves.

## V SHAPE

**1**

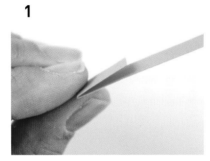

Fold a paper strip at the desired point.

**2**

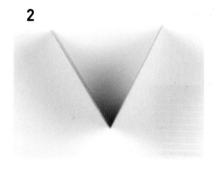

Cut the opposite side to make the ends even.

## ASYMMETRIC V SHAPE

Make a V shape (see above), but cut the opposite side to a different length so that you create an asymmetric V shape.

## ZIGZAG SHAPE

**1**

Start folding a paper strip as if you are making a V shape (see page 13), but instead of cutting the opposite side, continue folding along the same length.

**2**

When you finish making the folds, trim the end of the paper strip with a pair of scissors.

## ALMOND SHAPE

**1**

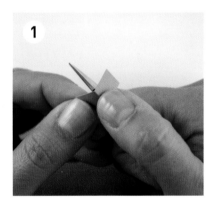

Start by making a V shape (see page 13).

**2**

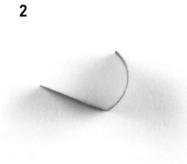

Run the edge of a pair of scissors from the folding point to the end of the strip to curve it towards one side, as shown here. Repeat for the opposite side.

**3**

Apply a thin layer of glue to the edge of one end of the strip.

**4**

Stick to the other side using your fingers. This will create an almond shape.

## MARQUISE SHAPE

**1**

Make a coil (see page 10). Without applying glue, flatten it gently by squeezing it with your fingers.

**2**

This will create a marquise shape.

**3**

Apply a thin layer of glue to the end of the paper strip to seal it to the shape and leave to dry.

## DIAMOND SHAPE

**1**

Create a marquise shape (see above). Holding it at the pointed ends, press gently from both sides.

**2**

Holding the flattened shape with a pair of tweezers, apply a thin layer of glue to the end of the paper strip.

**3**

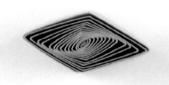

Stick the end of the paper to the diamond shape and leave to dry.

# MARQUISE SHAPE COVERED WITH PAPER

**1**

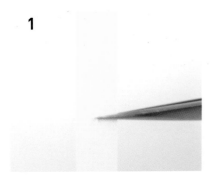

Make a marquise shape (see page 15). Apply glue to the end of a different-coloured strip of paper.

**2**

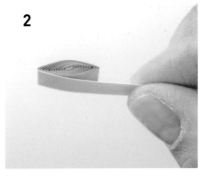

Glue the end of the strip onto the marquise shape you just prepared.

**3**

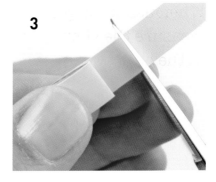

Wrap the rest of the strip around the marquise shape and cut it at the desired point.

**4**

Apply a thin layer of glue to the end of the paper strip.

**5**

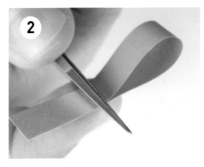

Secure the end of the paper to the marquise shape and leave to dry.

## BENT DROP SHAPE

**1**

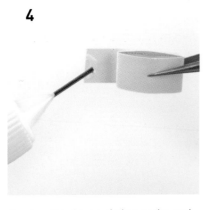

Glue the facing edges of a paper strip together at the ends.

**2**

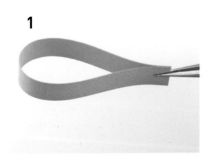

Run the edge of a pair of scissors about halfway along towards the ends of the paper strip.

**3**

You should now have a curve, creating a bent drop shape.

# Measuring and placing shapes

When using templates and outlines for quilling, it is useful to know how to measure the shapes so that they are the correct size and length for placing in the outline. The cloud template is used in the example below.

**1**

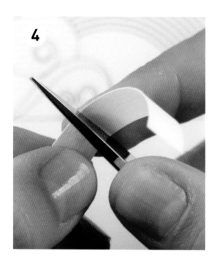

Position the finished paper shape over the corresponding shape on the template.

**2**

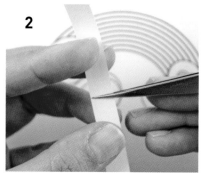

At the point where the strip meets the end of the template, mark it by using a pair of tweezers to create a bend in the strip.

**3**

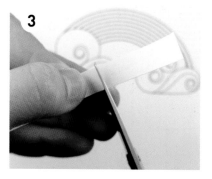

Cut the excess paper away using a pair of scissors.

**4**

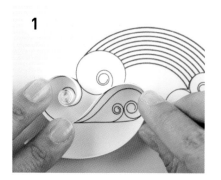

Bend the shape if necessary to make sure it exactly follows the line on the template.

**5**

To check that you are happy with how the shape fits, before adding any glue, place the shape in the outline in the same position as shown on the template.

**6**

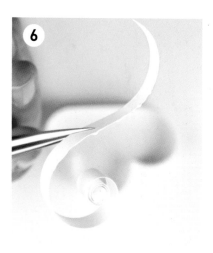

Holding the shape with a pair of tweezers, apply a thin layer of glue to the bottom of the shape along the edges of the paper. Use the tweezers to place it into your outline. Press down lightly with your finger to secure it. Leave to dry.

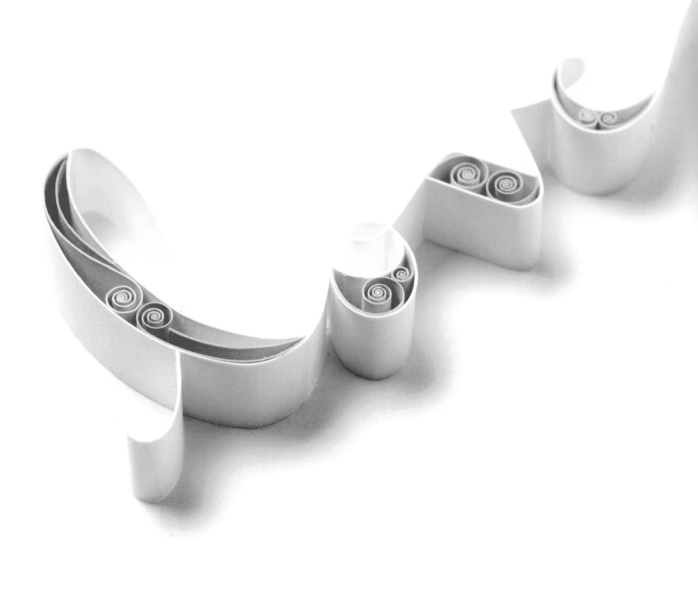

# Love

Here lettering is combined with quilling that uses several colours and shapes to produce a simple yet elegant creation that would make a fabulous wedding gift.

## materials

- Template on page 146

- Blank sheet of 90lb (250gsm) cardstock

- ⅜in (1cm) strips of 90lb (250gsm) cardstock

- 11 x ⅜in (28 x 1cm) light pink paper x 1

- 11 x ⅜in (28 x 1cm) salmon pink paper x 1

## tools

- Scissors

- Tweezers

- White glue

- Quilling tool (optional)

**1**

To create your base, place a sheet of blank cardstock under the template, then trace the outline onto it (see page 8). (Here, the outline has been darkened for clarity.)

**2**

Use strips of cardstock to prepare the outline (see page 8).

**3**

Make an asymmetric scroll using a light pink strip (see page 12).

**4**

Apply a thin layer of glue to the bottom of the scroll and place it in the upper section of the letter 'L', with the end of the strip curving from the right up towards the left.

**5**

Slightly bend a salmon pink strip as shown.

**6**

Apply a thin layer of glue to the bottom of the strip and place it to the right of the asymmetric scroll.

**7**

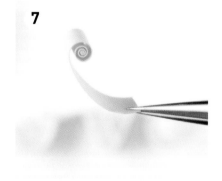

Make an open coil using a salmon pink strip (see page 11).

**8**

Apply a thin layer of glue to the bottom of the coil and place it under the asymmetric scroll, with the end of the strip running down the left-hand side.

**9**

Slightly bend a light pink strip, as shown.

**10**

Apply a thin layer of glue to the bottom of the shape and place it in the bottom of the letter 'L' below the salmon pink open coil.

**11**

Make an open coil using a light pink strip.

**12**

Apply a thin layer of glue to the bottom of the coil and place it inside the letter 'O', with the end of the strip on the left-hand side.

**13**

Make a smaller open coil using a salmon pink strip.

**14**

Apply a thin layer of glue to the bottom of the coil and place it inside the letter 'O' to the right of the light pink strip and with the end of the strip on the right-hand side.

**15**

Make an open coil using a light pink strip.

**16**

Apply a thin layer of glue to the bottom of the coil and place it in the top left section of the letter 'V', with the end of the strip at the top and curving from right to left.

**17**

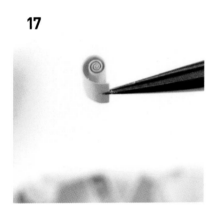

Using a salmon pink strip, make an open coil the same size as the one in step 15.

**18**

Apply a thin layer of glue to the bottom of the coil and place it in the bottom left section of the letter 'V', below the light pink coil and with the end of the strip at the bottom, curving from left to right.

**19**

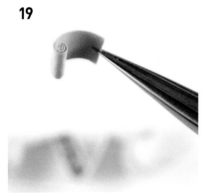

Make a smaller open coil using a light pink strip.

**20**

Apply a thin layer of glue to the bottom of the coil and place it inside the letter 'E', with the end of the strip on top and on the left-hand side.

**21**

Make a smaller open coil using a salmon pink strip.

**22**

Apply a thin layer of glue to the bottom of the coil and place it inside the letter 'E', below the light pink coil, with the end of the strip extending from left to right.

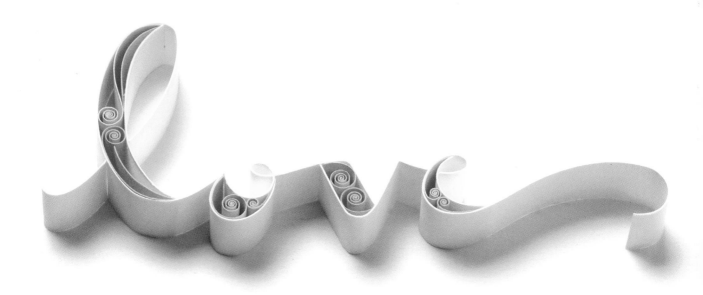

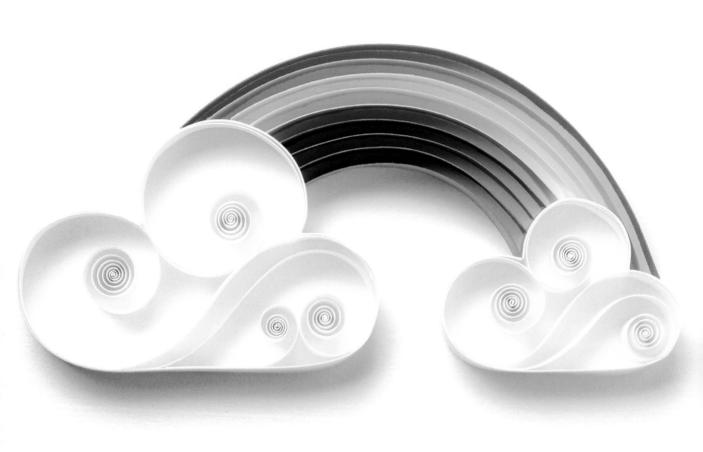

# Rainbow

This lovely, colourful rainbow nestling behind snow-white clouds is an easy project to make, but at the same time it will look impressive.

## materials

- Template on page 149
- Blank sheet of 90lb (250gsm) cardstock
- ⅜in (1cm) strips of 90lb (250gsm) cardstock
- 11 x ⅜in (28 x 1cm) purple paper x 1
- 11 x ⅜in (28 x 1cm) dark blue paper x 1
- 11 x ⅜in (28 x 1cm) blue paper x 1
- 11 x ⅜in (28 x 1cm) green paper x 1
- 11 x ⅜in (28 x 1cm) light green paper x 1
- 11 x ⅜in (28 x 1cm) light yellow paper x 1
- 11 x ⅜in (28 x 1cm) yellow paper x 1
- 11 x ⅜in (28 x 1cm) orange paper x 1
- 11 x ⅜in (28 x 1cm) red paper x 1
- 11 x ⅜in (28 x 1cm) white paper x 3

## tools

- Scissors
- Tweezers
- White glue
- Quilling tool (optional)

**1**

To create your base, place a sheet of blank cardstock under the template, then trace the outline onto it (see page 8). (Here, the outline has been darkened for clarity.)

**2**

Use strips of cardstock to prepare the outlines of the two clouds (see page 8).

**3**

Slightly bend a purple strip, as shown.

**4**

Apply a thin layer of glue to the bottom of the strip and place it between the two clouds.

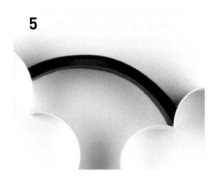

**5**

Slightly bend a dark blue strip. Apply a thin layer of glue to the bottom of the strip and place it above the purple strip.

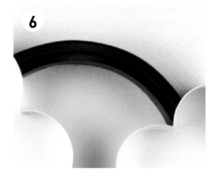

**6**

Slightly bend a blue strip. Apply a thin layer of glue to the bottom of the strip and place it above the dark blue strip.

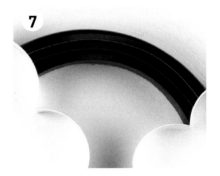

**7**

Slightly bend a green strip. Apply a thin layer of glue to the bottom of the strip and place it above the blue strip.

**8**

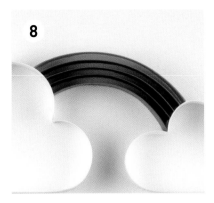

Slightly bend a light green strip. Apply a thin layer of glue to the bottom of the strip and place it above the green strip.

**9**

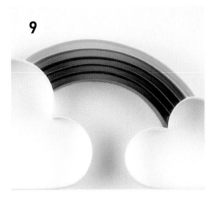

Slightly bend a light yellow strip. Apply a thin layer of glue to the bottom of the strip and place it above the light green strip.

**10**

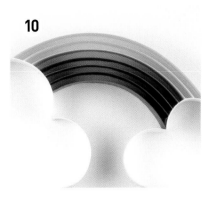

Slightly bend a yellow strip. Apply a thin layer of glue to the bottom of the strip and place it above the light yellow strip.

**11**

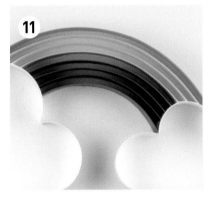

Slightly bend an orange strip. Apply a thin layer of glue to the bottom of the strip and place it above the yellow strip.

**12**

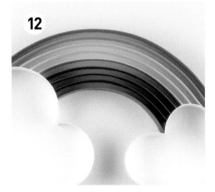

Slightly bend a red strip. Apply a thin layer of glue to the bottom of the strip and place it above the orange strip.

**13**

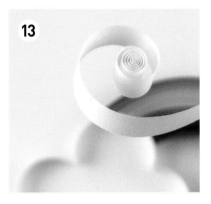

Make an asymmetric scroll using a white strip (see page 12).

**14**

Apply a thin layer of glue to the bottom of the scroll and place it in the bottom left section of the left-hand cloud, with the end of the strip extending from the bottom up towards the right.

**15**

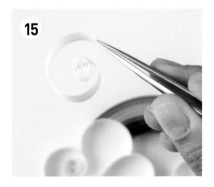

Make an open coil using a white strip (see page 11).

**16**

Apply a thin layer of glue to the bottom of the coil and place it in the top section of the left-hand cloud, with the end of the strip extending from the bottom towards the left.

**17**

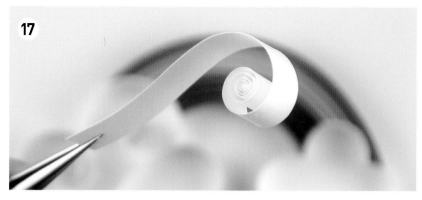

Make another asymmetric scroll using a white strip.

**18**

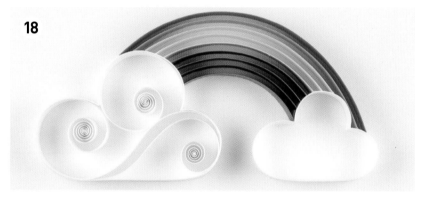

Apply a thin layer of glue to the bottom of the scroll and place it in the bottom right section of the left-hand cloud, with the long strip extending from the right, upwards and then down to the left.

**19**

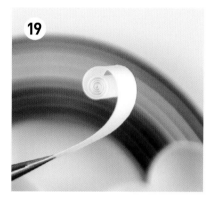

Make a smaller open coil using a white strip.

**20**

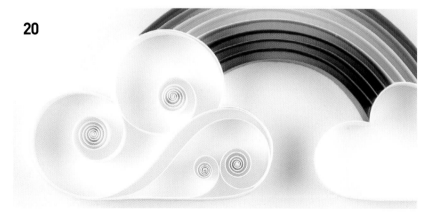

Apply a thin layer of glue to the bottom of the coil and place it to the left of the scroll placed in step 18, with the end of the strip at the bottom, extending from right to left.

**21**

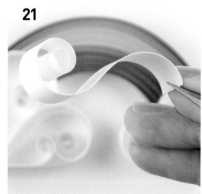

Make an asymmetric scroll using a white strip.

**22**

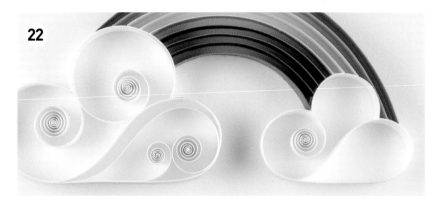

Apply a thin layer of glue to the bottom of the scroll and place it in the bottom left section of the right-hand cloud, with the end of the strip extending from the bottom up towards the right.

**23**

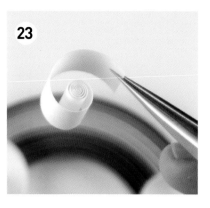

Make an open coil using a white strip.

**24**

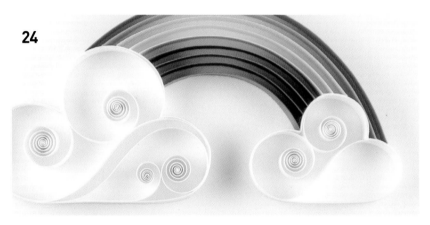

Apply a thin layer of glue to the bottom of the coil and place it in the top section of the right-hand cloud, with the end of the strip extending from the bottom towards the left.

**25**

Make an asymmetric coil using a white strip.

**26**

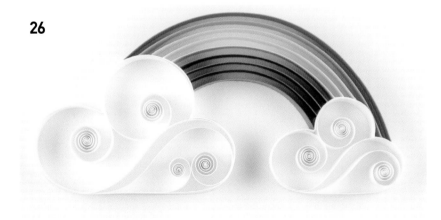

Apply a thin layer of glue to the bottom of the scroll and place it in the bottom right section of the right-hand cloud, with the end of the strip extending from the right, upwards and then down to the left.

# Tree

Bring nature into your home with this stunning tree. Varying shades of green depict a tree in full leaf, but you could make the leaves from autumnal colours instead.

## materials

- Template on page 148
- Blank sheet of 90lb (250gsm) cardstock
- 11 x ⅜in (28 x 1cm) brown paper x 2
- 11 x ⅜in (28 x 1cm) light brown paper x 4
- 11 x ⅜in (28 x 1cm) lime paper x 2
- 11 x ⅜in (28 x 1cm) seafoam paper x 1
- 11 x ⅜in (28 x 1cm) green paper x 2
- 11 x ⅜in (28 x 1cm) emerald paper x 1
- 11 x ⅜in (28 x 1cm) seaweed paper x 1

## tools

- Scissors
- Tweezers
- White glue
- Quilling tool (optional)

**1**

To create your base, place a sheet of blank cardstock under the template, then trace the outline onto it (see page 8). (Here, the outline has been darkened for clarity.)

**2**

Use strips of brown paper to prepare the outline of the tree (see page 8).

**3**

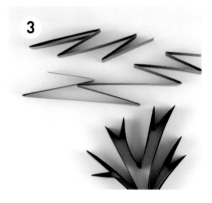

To fill the body and the branches of the tree, make random zigzag shapes (see page 14) using light brown strips.

**4**

Apply a thin layer of glue to the bottom of the shapes and place them inside the trunk and branches of the tree (you can place them as you want – it is not necessary to position them exactly as shown).

**5**

Make almond shapes for the leaves (see page 14), with each colour being smaller than the previous one: 11 leaves from lime paper, 9 from seafoam paper, 16 from green paper, 6 from emerald paper and 8 from seaweed paper.

**6**

One at a time, apply a thin layer of glue to the bottom of the shapes and place one seaweed leaf, two green leaves, two seafoam leaves and two lime leaves on the bottom left branch.

**7**

One at a time, apply a thin layer of glue to the bottom of the shapes and place one seaweed leaf, two green leaves, one seafoam leaf and one lime leaf below the centre left branch.

**8**

One at a time, apply a thin layer of glue to the bottom of the shapes and place one seaweed leaf, one emerald leaf, one green leaf and one lime leaf above the centre left branch.

**9**

One at a time, apply a thin layer of glue to the bottom of the shapes and place two green leaves, one seafoam leaf and two lime leaves towards the top left-hand side of the top left branch.

**10**

One at a time, apply a thin layer of glue to the bottom of the shapes and place one seaweed leaf, one green leaf, one seafoam leaf and one lime leaf to the right-hand side of the top left branch.

**11**

One at a time, apply a thin layer of glue to the bottom of the shapes and place one seaweed leaf, one emerald leaf, one green leaf, one seafoam leaf and one lime leaf above the top right branch.

**12**

One at a time, apply a thin layer of glue to the bottom of the shapes and place two emerald leaves, one green leaf and one lime leaf to the right-hand side of the top right branch.

**13**

One at a time, apply a thin layer of glue to the bottom of the shapes and place one seaweed leaf, two green leaves and one seafoam leaf to the right of the centre right branch.

**14**

One at a time, apply a thin layer of glue to the bottom of the shapes and place one emerald leaf, one green leaf and one lime leaf below the centre right branch.

**15**

One at a time, apply a thin layer of glue to the bottom of the shapes and place two seaweed leaves, one emerald leaf, three green leaves, two seafoam leaves and one lime leaf around the bottom right branch.

Make a small open coil using an emerald strip (see page 11). Apply a thin layer of glue to the bottom of the coil and place it inside the seafoam leaf below the bottom left branch.

Make a small open coil using a green strip. Apply a thin layer of glue to the bottom of the coil and place it inside the lime leaf above the bottom left branch.

Slightly bend a small piece of seafoam strip. Apply a thin layer of glue to the bottom of the strip and place it inside the lime leaf below the centre left branch.

Slightly bend a small piece of lime strip. Apply a thin layer of glue to the bottom of the strip and place it inside the emerald leaf above the centre left branch.

Make a small open coil using an emerald strip. Apply a thin layer of glue to the bottom of the coil and place it inside the lime leaf at the tip of the centre left branch.

Make a small open coil using a lime strip. Apply a thin layer of glue to the bottom of the coil and place it inside the seafoam leaf on the left-hand side of the top left branch.

Slightly bend a small piece of green strip. Apply a thin layer of glue to the bottom of the strip and place it inside the lime leaf above the top left branch.

Make a small open coil using a lime strip. Apply a thin layer of glue to the bottom of the coil and place it inside the green leaf on the left-hand side above the top right branch.

Slightly bend a small piece of lime strip. Apply a thin layer of glue to the bottom of the strip and place it inside the seaweed leaf on the right-hand side above the top right branch.

**25**

Make a small open coil using an emerald strip. Apply a thin layer of glue to the bottom of the coil and place it inside the lime leaf on the left side of the centre right branch.

**26**

Make a small open coil using a lime strip. Apply a thin layer of glue to the bottom of the coil and place it inside the green leaf to the right of the centre right branch.

**27**

Slightly bend a small piece of seafoam strip. Apply a thin layer of glue to the bottom of the strip and place it inside the lime leaf below the centre right branch.

**28**

Slightly bend a small piece of lime strip. Apply a thin layer of glue to the bottom of the strip and place it inside the emerald leaf above the bottom right branch.

**29**

Make a small open coil using a green strip. Apply a thin layer of glue to the bottom of the coil and place it inside the seaweed leaf on the right-hand side above the bottom right branch.

**30**

Make a small open coil using a green strip. Apply a thin layer of glue to the bottom of the strip and place it inside the seafoam leaf at the far right of the bottom right branch.

# Cheesecake

Quilling coils and different coloured drawings are combined in this project to make an attractive kitchen decoration.

## materials

- Template on page 147

- Blank sheet of 90lb (250gsm) cardstock

- 11 x ⅜in (28 x 1cm) strips of 90lb (250gsm) cardstock

- 11 x ⅜in (28 x 1cm) peanut paper x 3

- 11 x ⅜in (28 x 1cm) cream paper x 3

- 11 x ⅜in (28 x 1cm) red paper x 2

- Blank sheet of A4/US letter-size paper

## tools

- Scissors

- Tweezers

- White glue

- Quilling tool (optional)

- Black, red and green marker pens

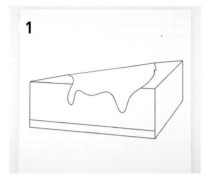

**1**

To create your base, place a sheet of blank cardstock under the template, then trace the outline onto it (see page 8). (Here, the outline has been darkened for clarity.)

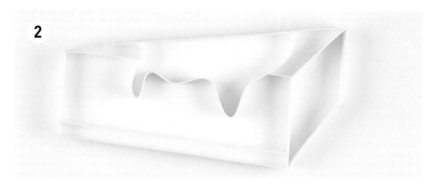

**2**

Use strips of cardstock to prepare the outline of the cheesecake (see page 8).

**3**

Make a coil using a peanut strip (see page 10). Apply a thin layer of glue to the bottom of the coil and place it on right-hand side of the cake, in the back of the slice.

**4**

Make a smaller coil using a peanut strip. Apply a thin layer of glue to the bottom of the coil and place it below the previous one, as shown.

**5**

Make a smaller coil using a peanut strip. Apply a thin layer of glue to the bottom of the coil and place it below the coil applied in step 4.

**6**

Make a small coil using a peanut strip. Apply a thin layer of glue to the bottom of the coil and place it above the biggest coil.

**7**

Make a smaller coil using a peanut strip. Apply a thin layer of glue to the bottom of the coil and place it above the coil applied in step 6.

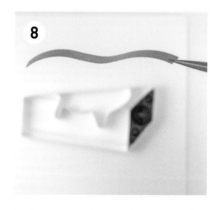

**8**

Make a wave shape using a peanut strip (see page 13).

**9**

Apply a thin layer of glue to the bottom of the shape and place it at the bottom of the cheesecake.

**10**

Make another wave shape using a peanut strip. Apply a thin layer of glue to the bottom of the shape and place it below the wave shape applied in step 8.

**11**

Slightly bend a peanut strip. Apply a thin layer of glue to the bottom of the strip and place it centred above the two wave shapes.

**12**

Using a cream strip, make a C scroll (see page 12), but bend the strip in the centre as shown.

**13**

Apply a thin layer of glue to the bottom of the scroll and place it as shown in the side section of the cheesecake, with the larger scroll on the left-hand side.

**14**

Make an asymmetric scroll using a cream strip (see page 12). Apply a thin layer of glue to the bottom of the scroll and place it below the bend in the C scroll, with the end of the strip curving from the top downwards to the left.

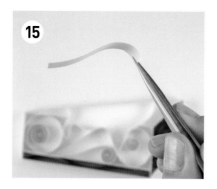

**15**

Bend a cream strip as shown.

**16**

Apply a thin layer of glue to the bottom of the strip and place it above the asymmetric scroll applied in step 14.

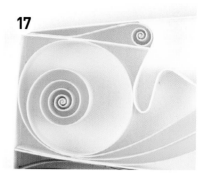

**17**

Make a smaller asymmetric scroll using a cream strip. Apply a thin layer of glue to the bottom of the scroll and place it on the left side of the top of the slice.

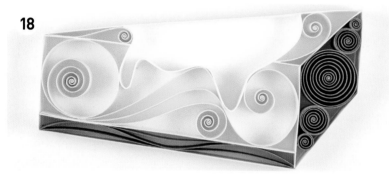

**18**

Make an open coil using a cream strip (see page 11). Apply a thin layer of glue to the bottom of the coil and place it on the right-hand side of the top of the slice.

**19**

For the cheesecake topping, make the shape as shown using a red strip, forming a deep curve in the centre and with the left end having a simple slight curve.

**20**

Apply a thin layer of glue to the bottom of the shape and place it at the top of the slice, with the wave shape in the strip following the outline on the right-hand side and the deep curve towards the bottom.

**21**

Make an open coil using a red strip. Apply a thin layer of glue to the bottom of the coil and place it under the left-hand end of the strip applied in step 20, with the end curving to the left.

**22**

Make an asymmetric scroll using a red strip. Apply a thin layer of glue to the bottom of the scroll and place it above the strip applied in step

20, with the coil in the centre and the end of the strip extending from below to the left.

**23**

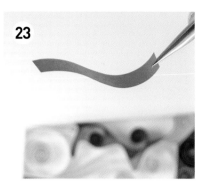

Bend a red strip as shown.

**24**

Apply a thin layer of glue to the bottom of the strip and place it above the other red strips, as shown.

**25**

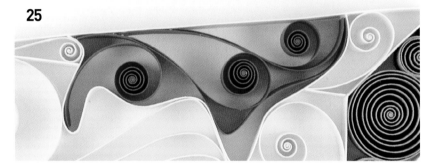

Make an asymmetric scroll using a red strip. Apply a thin layer of glue to the bottom of the scroll and place it above the other red strips,

with the coil towards the right and the end of the strip extending from below to the left.

**26**

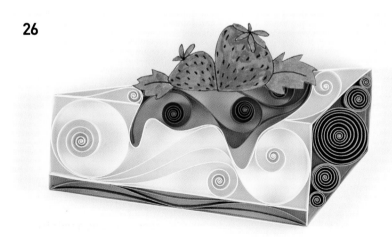

Referring to the template, draw the strawberries and leaves on a blank sheet of paper and colour them in.

Cut out the shape, apply a thin layer of glue to the back of the paper and place it on top.

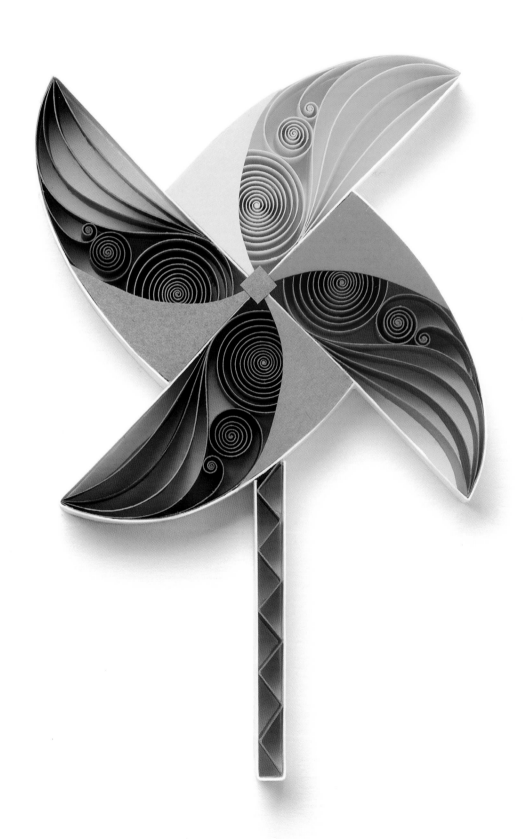

# Pinwheel

Repeating patterns and different colours create the illusion of a moving image in this quilling version of a child's toy.

## materials

- Template on page 146
- Blank sheet of 90lb (250gsm) cardstock
- ⅜in (1cm) strips of 90lb (250gsm) cardstock
- 11 x ⅜in (28 x 1cm) yellow paper x 2
- 11 x ⅜in (28 x 1cm) red paper x 2
- 11 x ⅜in (28 x 1cm) green paper x 2
- 11 x ⅜in (28 x 1cm) blue paper x 2
- 11 x ⅜in (28 x 1cm) dark yellow paper x 1
- 11 x ⅜in (28 x 1cm) dark red paper x 1
- 11 x ⅜in (28 x 1cm) dark green paper x 1
- 11 x ⅜in (28 x 1cm) dark blue paper x 1
- 1¼ x 1¼in (3 x 3cm) paper in yellow, red, green and blue x 1 of each
- 11 x ⅜in (28 x 1cm) dark grey paper x 1

## tools

- Scissors
- Tweezers
- White glue
- Quilling tool (optional)

**1**

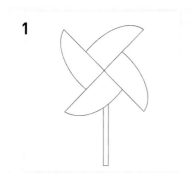

To create your base, place a sheet of blank cardstock under the template, then trace the outline onto it (see page 8). (Here, the outline has been darkened for clarity.)

**2**

Use strips of cardstock to prepare the outline (see page 8).

**3**

Make an asymmetric scroll using a yellow strip (see page 12).

**4**

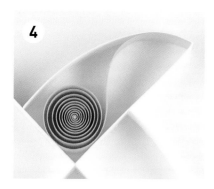

Apply a thin layer of glue to the bottom of the scroll and place it in the top right section of the pinwheel, with the end of the strip on the right and ending at the point.

**5**

Make another asymmetric scroll using a red strip. Apply glue to the bottom of the scroll and place it in the bottom right section, with the end at the bottom and ending at the point.

**6**

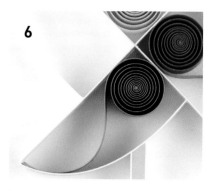

Make another asymmetric scroll using a green strip. Apply glue to the bottom of the scroll and place it in the bottom left section, with the end of the strip on the left and ending at the point.

**7**

Make another asymmetric scroll using a blue strip. Apply glue to the bottom of the scroll and place it in the top left section, with the end at the top and ending at the point.

**8**

Make an open coil using a dark yellow strip (see page 11).

**9**

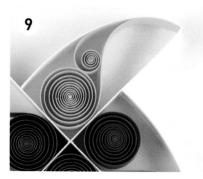

Apply a thin layer of glue to the bottom of the coil. Place it above the yellow scroll, with the end of the strip on the left-hand side.

**10**

Make a smaller open coil using a dark yellow strip.

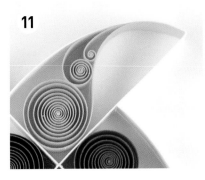

**11**

Apply a thin layer of glue to the bottom of the coil and place it above the two yellow scrolls, with the end of the strip on the left-hand side.

**12**

Make an open coil using a dark red strip. Apply a thin layer of glue to the bottom of the coil and place it to the right of the dark red scroll, with the end of the strip on top.

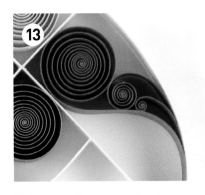

**13**

Make a smaller open coil using a dark red strip. Apply a thin layer of glue to the bottom of the coil and place it to the right of the red scrolls, with the end of the strip on top.

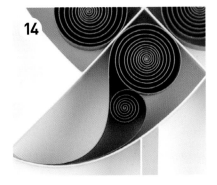

**14**

Make an open coil using a dark green strip. Apply a thin layer of glue to the bottom of the coil and place it below the green scroll, with the end of the strip extending from the right.

**15**

Make a smaller open coil using a dark green strip. Apply a thin layer of glue to the bottom of the coil and place it below the two green scrolls, with the end of the strip at the bottom.

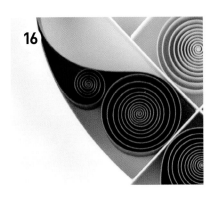

**16**

Make an open coil using a dark blue strip. Apply a thin layer of glue to the bottom of the coil and place it to the left of the blue scroll, with the end of the strip extending to the left.

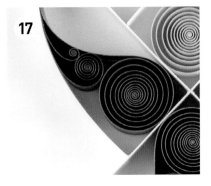

**17**

Make a smaller open coil using a dark blue strip. Apply a thin layer of glue to the bottom and place it to the left of the blue scrolls, with the end of the strip extending to the left.

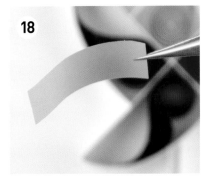

**18**

Make an asymmetric wave shape using a yellow strip (see page 13).

**19**

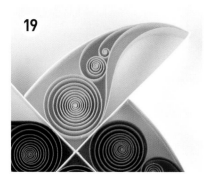

Apply a thin layer of glue to the bottom of the shape and place it to the right of the three yellow scrolls.

**20**

Make an asymmetric wave shape using a red strip. Apply a thin layer of glue to the bottom of the shape and place it below the red scrolls.

**21**

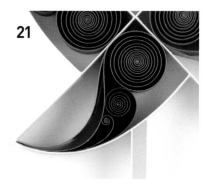

Make an asymmetric wave shape using a green strip. Apply a thin layer of glue to the bottom and place it to the left of the green scrolls.

**22**

Make an asymmetric wave shape using a blue strip. Apply a thin layer of glue to the bottom of the shape and place it above the blue scrolls.

**23**

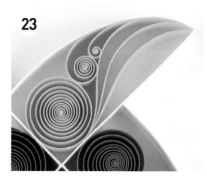

Make an asymmetric wave shape using a dark yellow strip. Apply a thin layer of glue to the bottom of the shape and place it to the right of the yellow wave shape.

**24**

Make an asymmetric wave shape using a dark red strip. Apply a thin layer of glue to the bottom of the shape and place it below the red wave shape.

**25**

Make an asymmetric wave shape using a dark green strip. Apply a thin layer of glue to the bottom of the shape and place it to the left of the green wave shape.

**26**

Make an asymmetric wave shape using a dark blue strip. Apply a thin layer of glue to the bottom of the shape and place it above the blue wave shape.

**27**

Slightly bend a yellow strip. Apply a thin layer of glue to the bottom of the strip and place it to the right of the yellow wave shapes.

**28**

Slightly bend a red strip. Apply a thin layer of glue to the bottom of the strip and place it below the red wave shapes.

**29**

Slightly bend a green strip. Apply a thin layer of glue to the bottom of the strip and place it to the left of the green wave shapes.

**30**

Slightly bend a blue strip. Apply a thin layer of glue to the bottom of the strip and place it above the blue wave shapes.

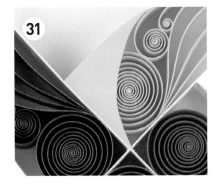

**31**

Using the template on page 146 and the yellow section of the image above as a guide, cut a triangle with a curved edge from yellow paper. Apply a thin layer of glue to the back of the shape and place it as shown.

**32**

Repeat step 31 but cut the triangle from red paper. Apply a thin layer of glue to the back of the shape and place it in the red section, as shown.

**33**

Repeat step 31 but cut the triangle from green paper. Apply a thin layer of glue to the back of the shape and place it in the green section, as shown.

**34**

Repeat step 31 but cut the triangle from blue paper. Apply a thin layer of glue to the back of the shape and place it in the blue section, as shown.

**35**

Using a dark grey strip, prepare a zigzag shape (see page 14). Apply a thin layer of glue to the bottom of the shape and place it in the vertical rectangle (the pinwheel's rod).

**36**

Cut a small square from dark grey paper. Apply a thin layer of glue to the back of the square and place it in the centre of the pinwheel, as shown.

# Ice cream

Asymmetric scrolls, waves and classic coils are used here to create an ice cream that looks good enough to eat.

## materials

- Template on page 147
- Blank sheet of 90lb (250gsm) cardstock
- 11 x ⅜in (28 x 1cm) ochre paper x 6
- 11 x ⅜in (28 x 1cm) yellow paper x 1
- 11 x ⅜in (28 x 1cm) amber paper x 1
- 11 x ⅜in (28 x 1cm) light yellow paper x 1
- 11 x ⅜in (28 x 1cm) orange paper x 1
- 11 x ⅜in (28 x 1cm) pink paper x 1

## tools

- Scissors
- Tweezers
- White glue
- Quilling tool (optional)

**1**

To create your base, place a sheet of blank cardstock under the template, then trace the outline onto it (see page 8). (Here, the outline has been darkened for clarity.)

**2**

Use strips of cardstock to prepare the outline of the ice cream (see page 8).

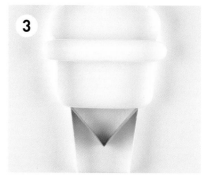

**3**

Make a V shape using an ochre strip (see page 13). Apply a thin layer of glue to the bottom of the shape. Place it in the bottom cone section, with the ends in the two top corners.

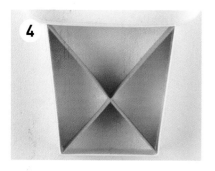

**4**

Make a smaller V shape using an ochre strip. Apply a thin layer of glue to the bottom of the shape and place below the previous shape, with the ends of the strip in the two bottom corners.

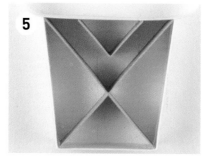

**5**

Make a smaller V shape using an ochre strip. Apply a thin layer of glue to the bottom of the shape and place it centred inside the V shape placed in step 3, with the ends of the strip along the top edge.

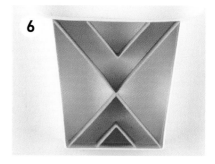

**6**

Make a smaller V shape using an ochre strip. Apply a thin layer of glue to the bottom of the shape and place it centered inside the V shape placed in step 4, with the ends of the strip along the bottom edge.

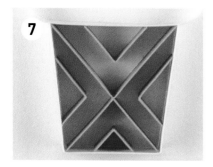

**7**

Make two asymmetric V shapes using an ochre strip (see page 13). One at a time, apply a thin layer of glue to the bottom of the shapes and place them, one on the left side and one on the right side.

**8**

Make an asymmetric scroll using an ochre strip (see page 12). Apply a thin layer of glue to the bottom of the scroll. Place it in the adjacent section of the cone, with the end of the strip curving down from above.

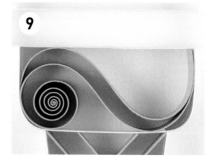

**9**

Make an S shape using an ochre strip (see page 12). Apply a thin layer of glue to the bottom of the shape and place it above the scroll, following the curve of the shape applied in step 8.

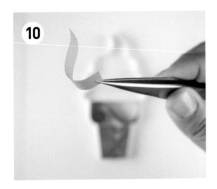

**10**

Make an asymmetric shape as shown, using an ochre strip – the technique is similar to making a wave shape (see page 13).

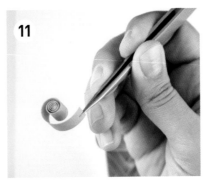

**11**

Make an open coil using an ochre strip (see page 11). Apply a thin layer of glue to the bottom of the two shapes.

**12**

Place the shapes above the step 9 shape, with the asymmetric shape following its curve on the left and the coil continuing it on the right, with the end curving up the right-hand side.

**13**

Make seven coils using ochre strips (see page 10). One at a time, apply a thin layer of glue to the bottom of the coils and place them in the top section of the cone.

**14**

Make an open coil using a yellow strip. Apply a thin layer of glue to the bottom of the coil. Place it with the coil in the middle tier of ice cream and the end of the strip curving from below right up to the tip.

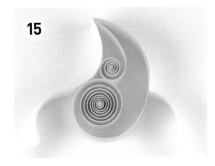

**15**

Make a smaller open coil using a yellow strip. Apply a thin layer of glue to the bottom of the coil and place it above the coil applied in step 14, with the end of the strip curving up to the tip.

**16**

Make a tight coil using a light yellow strip (see page 11). Apply a thin layer of glue to the bottom of the coil and place it just to the right of the coils applied in steps 14 and 15.

**17**

Make a C shape using an amber strip (see page 12). Apply a thin layer of glue to the bottom of the shape and place it under the coil applied in step 14, following its curve.

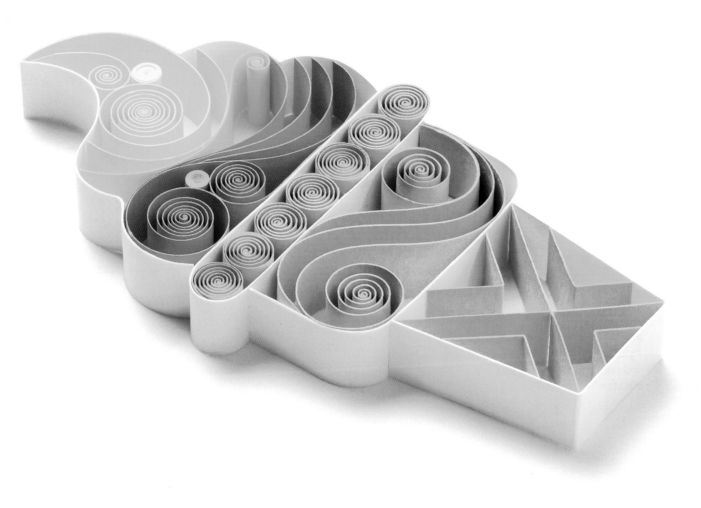

**18**

Make an asymmetric scroll using a pink strip. Apply a thin layer of glue to the bottom of the scroll. Place in the bottom of the ice cream, with the end of the strip curving from above the coil, down to the right and up.

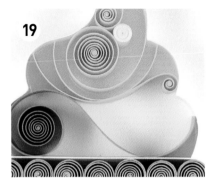

**19**

Make an asymmetric scroll using an amber strip. Apply a thin layer of glue to the bottom of the scroll. Place below the step 17 strip, with the end of the strip curving from above the coil, down to the left and up.

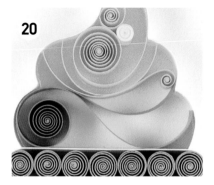

**20**

Make an asymmetric wave shape using an orange strip (see page 13). Apply a thin layer of glue to the bottom of the shape. Place it above the step 18 scroll, with the strip ending under the step 19 scroll.

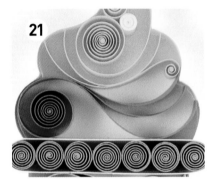

**21**

Make an asymmetric wave shape using an orange strip. Apply a thin layer of glue to the bottom of the shape and place it below the shape applied in step 20.

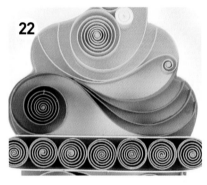

**22**

Make an asymmetric wave shape using a pink strip. Apply a thin layer of glue to the bottom of the shape and place it below the strip applied in step 21.

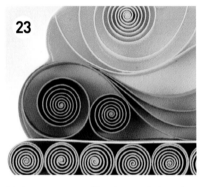

**23**

Make an open coil using a pink strip. Apply a thin layer of glue to the bottom of the coil. Place it below the step 22 shape, with the coil on the left and the end of the strip extending from the left and along the bottom.

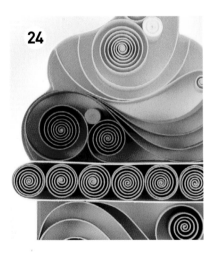

**24**

Make a tight coil using an orange strip. Apply a thin layer of glue to the bottom of the coil and place it near the top of the cone, between the coils applied in steps 18 and 23.

# Picnic basket

Only three different shades of yellow are used in this basket. To complete the image of a relaxing summertime picnic, there's a simple drawing for you to copy.

## materials

- Template on page 147
- Blank sheet of 90lb (250gsm) cardstock
- ⅜in (1cm) strips of 90lb (250gsm) cardstock
- 11 x ⅜in (28 x 1cm) yellow paper x 4
- 11 x ⅜in (28 x 1cm) amber paper x 3
- 11 x ⅜in (28 x 1cm) light yellow paper x 3

## tools

- Scissors
- Tweezers
- White glue
- Quilling tool (optional)
- Black, red, green, violet, purple and brown marker pens

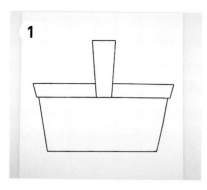

**1**

To create your base, place a sheet of blank cardstock under the template, then trace the outline onto it (see page 8). (Here, the outline has been darkened for clarity.)

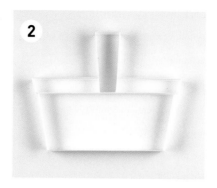

**2**

Use strips of cardstock to prepare the outline of the basket (see page 8).

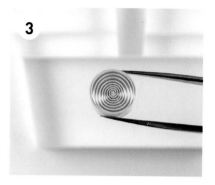

**3**

Make a coil using a yellow strip (see page 10).

**4**

Apply a thin layer of glue to the bottom of the strip and place it at the top of the handle.

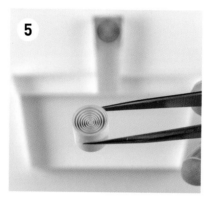

**5**

Make a smaller coil using a yellow strip.

**6**

Apply a thin layer of glue to the bottom of the coil and place it below the previous one.

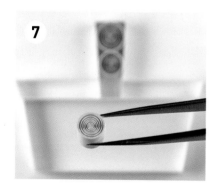

**7**

Make a smaller coil using a yellow strip.

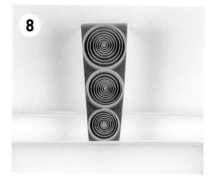

**8**

Apply a thin layer of glue to the bottom of the coil and place it below the previous one.

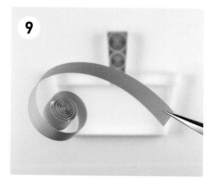

**9**

Make an open coil using an amber strip (see page 11).

**10**

Apply a thin layer of glue to the bottom of the coil and place it in the basket, with the coil at the left and the end of the strip on the left and curving upwards and down to the bottom right-hand corner.

**11**

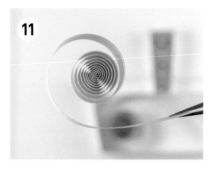

Make an open coil using a yellow strip.

**12**

Apply a thin layer of glue to the bottom of the coil. Place it to the right of the first coil, with the end of the strip curving from the top towards the left and then down to the bottom right-hand corner.

**13**

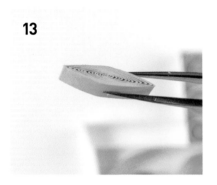

Make a marquise shape using an amber strip (see page 15).

**14**

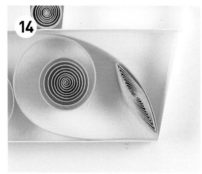

Apply a thin layer of glue to the bottom of the shape and place it in the right-hand corner, just below the end of the strip from the first coil.

**15**

Make another marquise shape using a yellow strip. Apply a thin layer of glue to the bottom of the strip and place it to the left of the previous one.

**16**

Make another marquise shape using a light yellow strip. Apply a thin layer of glue to the bottom of the shape and place it to the left of the previous one.

**17**

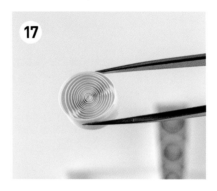

Make a coil using light a yellow strip.

**18**

Apply a thin layer of glue to the bottom of the coil and place it in the top right corner of the basket's main section.

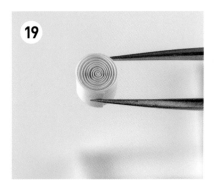

Make a smaller coil using a light yellow strip.

Apply a thin layer of glue to the bottom of the coil and place it to the left of the previous one.

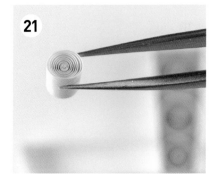

Make another smaller coil using a light yellow strip.

Apply a thin layer of glue to the bottom of the coil and place it below the large coil applied in step 18.

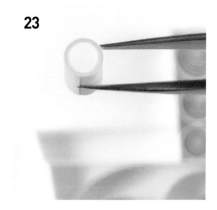

Make a tight coil using a light yellow strip and then cover it with an amber strip (see page 11).

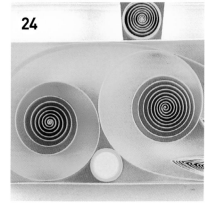

Apply a thin layer of glue to the bottom of the coil and place it at the bottom of the basket, between the two open coils.

Make a coil using a yellow strip.

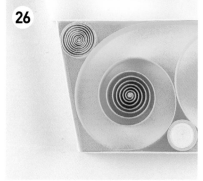

Apply a thin layer of glue to the bottom of the coil and place it in the top left corner of the basket's main section.

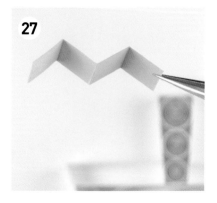

Make two zigzag shapes using a yellow strip (see page 14).

**28**

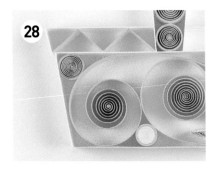

Apply a thin layer of glue to the bottom of one of the shapes and place it in the top left section of the basket, above the main section.

**29**

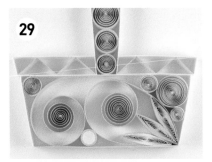

Apply a thin layer of glue to the bottom of the second zigzag shape and place it in the top right section.

**30**

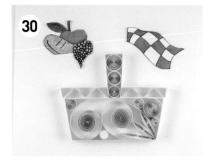

Use the template to draw the napkin and food items on a blank sheet of paper and colour them in. Cut out the shapes with a pair of scissors.

**31**

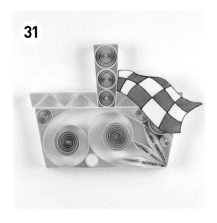

Apply a thin layer of glue to the back of the napkin and position it on the top right corner of the basket.

**32**

Apply a thin layer of glue to the back of the food items and position it along the top left corner of the basket.

# Jasmine

With creamy flowers and leaves made from different shades of green, this project will bring a suggestion of fresh floral scents to your room.

## materials

- Template on page 146
- Blank sheet of 90lb (250gsm) cardstock
- ⅜in (1cm) strips of 90lb (250gsm) cardstock
- 11 x ⅜in (28 x 1cm) cream paper x 2
- 11 x ⅜in (28 x 1cm) seaweed paper x 1
- 11 x ⅜in (28 x 1cm) emerald paper x 1
- 11 x ⅜in (28 x 1cm) seafoam paper x 1
- 11 x ⅜in (28 x 1cm) green paper x 1

## tools

- Scissors
- Tweezers
- White glue
- Quilling tool (optional)

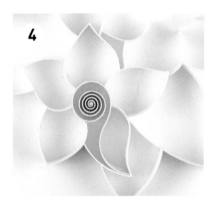

To create your base, place a sheet of blank cardstock under the template, then trace the outline onto it (see page 8). (Here, the outline has been darkened for clarity.)

Use strips of cardstock to prepare the outline (see page 8).

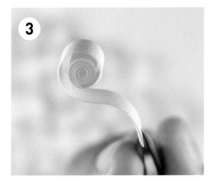

Make an asymmetric scroll using a cream strip (see page 12). Apply a thin layer of glue to the bottom of the scroll.

Place the scroll in the centre of the bottom flower, with the end of the strip extending from the right down to the point in the bottom right petal.

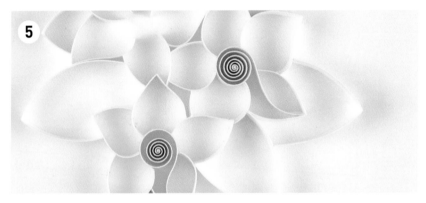

Make another asymmetric scroll using a cream strip. Apply glue to the bottom of the scroll and place it in the right-hand flower, with the end of the strip extending from the right to the point in the bottom right petal.

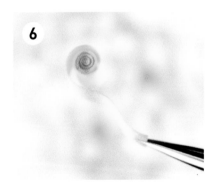

Make another asymmetric scroll using a cream strip, but add an extra bend on the tip.

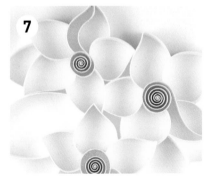

Apply a thin layer of glue to the bottom of the scroll and place it in the centre of the left-hand flower, with the end of the strip extending up from the right, as shown.

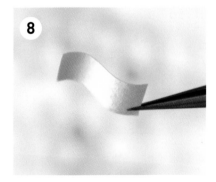

Make a wave shape using a cream strip (see page 13).

**9**

Apply a thin layer of glue to the bottom of the shape and place it in the top right-hand petal of the bottom flower.

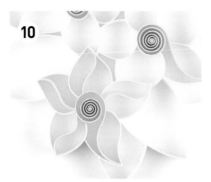

**10**

Make three wave shapes using cream strips. One at a time, apply a thin layer of glue to the bottom of the shapes and place them in the remaining three petals of the bottom flower.

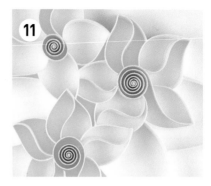

**11**

Make four wave shapes using cream strips. One at a time, apply a thin layer of glue to the bottom of the shapes and place them in the empty petals of the right-hand flower.

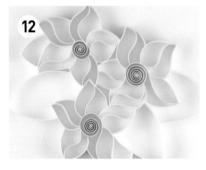

**12**

Make four wave shapes using cream strips. One at a time, apply a thin layer of glue to the bottom of the shapes and place them in the empty petals of the top left flower.

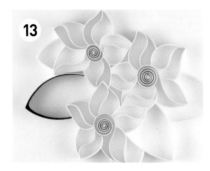

**13**

Apply a thin layer of glue to the bottom of a seaweed strip. Place it as shown inside the left-hand leaf, without a gap between it and the top and bottom of the outline.

**14**

Apply a thin layer of glue to the bottom of an emerald strip. Place it inside the same leaf, near the top edge.

**15**

Apply a thin layer of glue to the bottom of an emerald strip. Place it inside the same leaf, near the bottom edge.

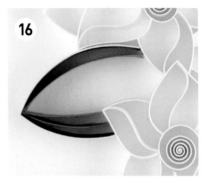

**16**

Apply a thin layer of glue to the bottom of an emerald strip. Place it inside the same leaf, just above the first emerald strip.

**17**

Apply a thin layer of glue to the bottom of a seafoam strip. Place it inside the same leaf, near the top edge.

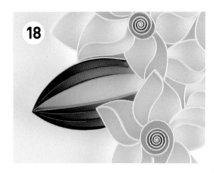

**18**

Apply a thin layer of glue to the bottom of a seafoam strip. Place it inside the same leaf, near the bottom edge.

**19**

Apply a thin layer of glue to the bottom of a green strip. Place it in the centre of the same leaf.

**20**

Apply a thin layer of glue to the bottom of an emerald strip. Place it as shown inside the top left leaf, without a gap between it and the top and bottom of the outline.

**21**

One at a time, apply a thin layer of glue to the bottom of two seafoam strips and place inside the same leaf, near the top and bottom edges.

**22**

Apply a thin layer of glue to the bottom of a green strip and place it in the centre of the same leaf.

**23**

Apply a thin layer of glue to a seaweed colour strip. Place it as shown inside the top right leaf, without a gap between it and the top and bottom of the outline.

**24**

One at a time, apply a thin layer of glue to the bottom of two emerald strips and place inside the same leaf, near the top and bottom edges.

**25**

One at a time, apply a thin layer of glue to the bottom of two green strips and place them inside the same leaf, near the strips applied in step 24.

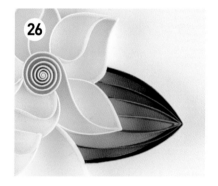

**26**

Apply a thin layer of glue to a seafoam strip and place it in the centre of the same leaf.

**27**

Apply a thin layer of glue to the bottom of a seaweed strip. Place it as shown inside the bottom right leaf, without a gap between it and the top and bottom of the outline.

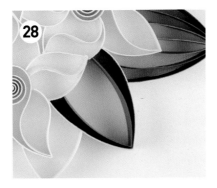

**28**

One at a time, apply a thin layer of glue to two emerald strips and place them inside the same leaf, near the top and bottom edges.

**29**

One at a time, apply a thin layer of glue to the bottom of two green strips and place them inside the same leaf, near the top and bottom edges.

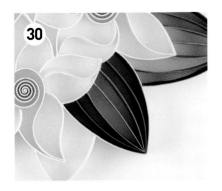

**30**

Apply a thin layer of glue to the bottom of a seafoam strip and place it in the centre of the same leaf.

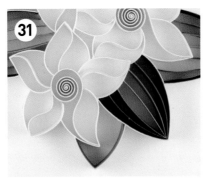

**31**

Apply a thin layer of glue to the bottom of an emerald strip. Place it as shown inside the bottom leaf, without a gap between it and the side edges of the outline.

**32**

One at a time, apply a thin layer of glue to the bottom of two green strips and place them inside the same leaf, near the side edges.

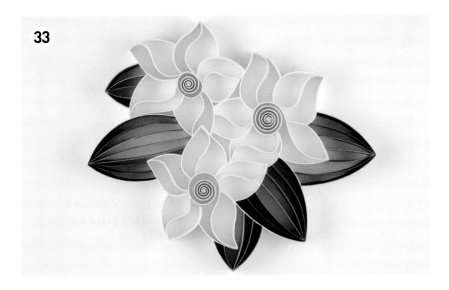

**33**

Apply a thin layer of glue to the bottom of a seafoam strip and place it in the same leaf, between the flower petal and the previously placed strip in the leaf's right-hand section.

# Swan

Create an elegant-looking swan by using an array of colours. Or why not make two swans so the pair can live a happy life together?

## materials

- Template on page 147
- Blank sheet of 90lb (250gsm) cardstock
- ⅜in (1cm) strips of 90lb (250gsm) cardstock
- 11 x ⅜in (28 x 1cm) light blue paper x 3
- 11 x ⅜in (28 x 1cm) mint paper x 2
- 11 x ⅜in (28 x 1cm) light green paper x 2
- 11 x ⅜in (28 x 1cm) cream paper x 2

## tools

- Scissors
- Tweezers
- White glue
- Quilling tool (optional)

**1**

To create your base, place a sheet of blank cardstock under the template, then trace the outline onto it (see page 8). (Here, the outline has been darkened for clarity.)

**2**

Use strips of cardstock to prepare the outline of the swan (see page 8).

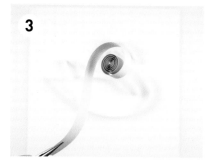

**3**

Make an asymmetric scroll using a light blue strip (see page 12).

**4**

Apply a thin layer of glue to the bottom of the scroll and place it in the bottom of the swan, with the scroll near the neck and the end of the strip curving up the right side and towards the left.

**5**

Make an S scroll, adapting the shape as shown here, using a mint strip (see page 12).

**6**

Apply a thin layer of glue to the bottom of the shape. Place it in the swan's neck, as shown, with the strip extending from below the smaller scroll to above the larger scroll near the base of the neck.

**7**

Make an open coil using a light green strip (see page 11). Apply a thin layer of glue to the bottom of the coil. Place it below the shape applied in step 6, with the end of the strip curving from below up the right side.

**8**

Make an open coil using a cream strip. Apply a thin layer of glue to the bottom of the coil. Place it between the shapes applied in steps 4 and 7, with the end of the strip curving from below up the right-hand side.

**9**

Make a tight coil using a light blue strip (see page 11). Apply a thin layer of glue to the bottom of the coil and place it as shown between the shapes applied in steps 4 and 8.

**10**

Make an asymmetric scroll using a mint strip. Apply a thin layer of glue to the bottom of the scroll. Place it above the shape applied in step 4, with the strip extending from below the scroll to the top right.

**11**

Make a wave shape using a cream strip (see page 13). Apply a thin layer of glue to the bottom of the shape.

Place it as shown between the shapes applied in steps 4 and 10.

**12**

Make another wave shape using a light green strip. Apply a thin layer of glue to the bottom of the shape and place it above the shape applied in step 11, following a similar curve.

**13**

Make a small open coil using a light green strip. Apply a thin layer of glue to the bottom of the coil. Place it to the left of the step 10 scroll, with the end of the strip extending from the right and along the bottom.

**14**

Make a smaller coil using a light green strip. Apply a thin layer of glue to the bottom of the coil and place it to the left of the coil applied in step 13.

**15**

Make a coil using a mint strip. Apply a thin layer of glue to the bottom of the coil and place it to the right of the scroll applied in step 10.

**16**

Make a smaller coil using a mint strip. Apply a thin layer of glue to the bottom of the coil and place it to the right of the scroll applied in step 15.

**17**

Make an open coil using a light green strip. Apply a thin layer of glue to the bottom of the coil. Place it to the left of the step 4 scroll, with the end of the strip extending down and along the bottom edge to the left.

**18**

Make a smaller open coil using a light blue strip. Apply a thin layer of glue to the bottom of the coil. Place it at the bottom between the two scrolls, with the end of the strip curving from below to the right.

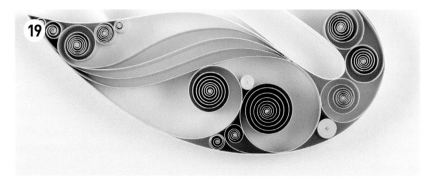

**19**

Make a smaller coil using a light blue strip. Apply a thin layer of glue to the bottom of the coil and place it to the left of the coil applied in step 18. Make a tight coil using a cream strip. Apply a thin layer of glue to the bottom of the coil and place it between the two scrolls applied in steps 4 and 17.

**20**

Make a C shape, adapting the shape as shown here, using a light green strip (see page 12).

**21**

Apply a thin layer of glue to the bottom of the strip and place it in the swan's neck to the right of the scroll applied in step 6.

**22**

Make a smaller open coil using a cream strip. Apply a thin layer of glue to the bottom of the coil and place it in the head above the step 6 S scroll, with the end of the strip curving from above to the left.

**23**

Make an asymmetric scroll using a cream strip. Apply a thin layer of glue to the bottom of the scroll. Place it in the neck to the left of the step 6 S scroll, with the end of the strip curving up and to the left.

**24**

Make a wave shape using a light blue strip. Apply a thin layer of glue to the bottom of the shape and place it in the bottom left corner of the far wing.

**25**

Make another wave shape using a cream strip. Apply a thin layer of glue to the bottom of the shape and place it above the wave shape applied in step 24, following its curve.

**26**

Make another wave shape using a light green strip. Apply a thin layer of glue to the bottom of the shape and place it above the wave shape placed in step 25.

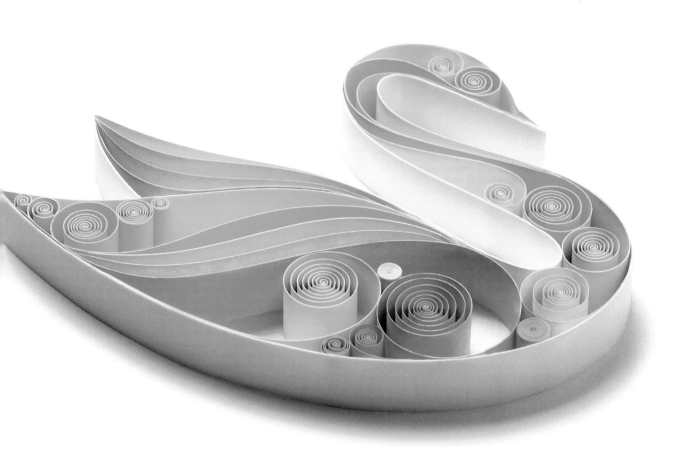

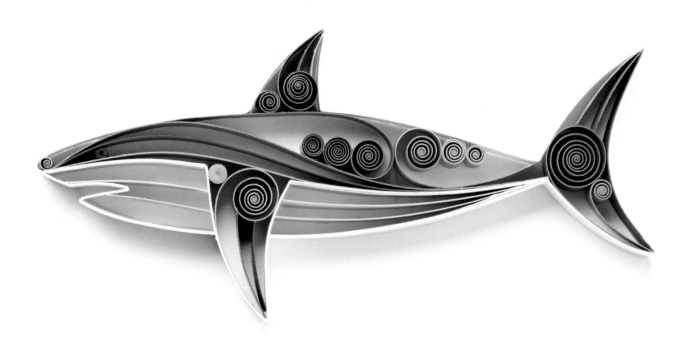

# Shark

To make this convincing shark, use paper strips in shades of blue and form them into coils and wave shapes.

## materials

- Template on page 150
- Blank sheet of 90lb (250gsm) cardstock
- ⅜in (1cm) strips of 90lb (250gsm) cardstock
- 11 x ⅜in (28 x 1cm) navy paper x 1
- 11 x ⅜in (28 x 1cm) azure paper x 2
- 11 x ⅜in (28 x 1cm) blue paper x 2
- 11 x ⅜in (28 x 1cm) light blue paper x 2
- 11 x ⅜in (28 x 1cm) black paper x 1

## tools

- Scissors
- Tweezers
- White glue
- Quilling tool (optional)

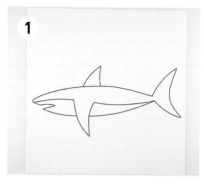

**1**

To create your base, place a sheet of blank cardstock under the template, then trace the outline onto it (see page 8). (Here, the outline has been darkened for clarity.)

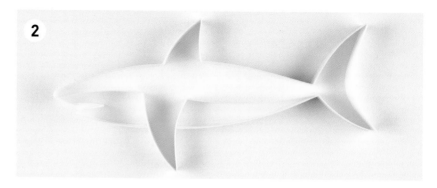

**2**

Use strips of cardstock to prepare the outline of the shark (see page 8).

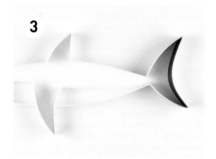

**3**

Slightly bend a piece of navy strip. Apply a thin layer of glue to the bottom of the strip and place it in the tail, leaving no gap between it and the cardstock on the right-hand side.

**4**

Make an open coil using an azure strip (see page 11). Apply a thin layer of glue to the bottom of the coil and place it in the centre of the shark's tail.

**5**

Make a smaller open coil using a blue strip. Apply a thin layer of glue to the bottom of the coil and place it below the larger coil, with the end of the strip curving from the left down to the tip of the tail.

**6**

Slightly bend a piece of azure strip. Apply a thin layer of glue to the bottom of the strip and place it in the tail, extending from above the large coil to the tip at the top of the tail.

**7**

Slightly bend a piece of blue strip. Apply a thin layer of glue to the bottom of the strip and place it inside the tail to the left of the strip applied in step 6.

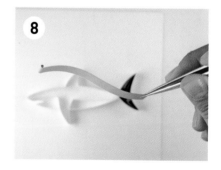

**8**

Make a shape based on an asymmetrical scroll using a blue strip (see page 12).

**9**

Apply a thin layer of glue to the bottom of the shape and place it in the top section of the shark's body, with the coil in the nose on the left and the end of strip curving from below to the tail on the right.

**10**

Make a wave shape using an azure strip (see page 13). Apply a thin layer of glue to the bottom of the shape and place it below the strip applied in step 9.

**11**

Make another wave shape using a blue strip. Apply a thin layer of glue to the bottom of the shape and place it below the strip applied in step 10.

**12**

Make an open coil using a blue strip. Apply a thin layer of glue to the bottom of the coil and place it above the step 8 shape, with the end of the strip curving from below towards the right.

**13**

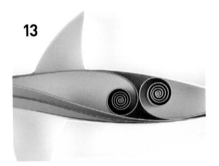

Make another open coil using an azure strip. Apply a thin layer of glue to the bottom of the coil and place it to the left of the step 12 coil, with the end of the strip curving up and towards the left.

**14**

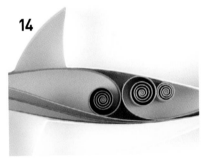

Make a coil using a blue strip (see page 10). Apply a thin layer of glue to the bottom of the coil and place it to the right of the coil applied in step 12.

**15**

Make a smaller coil using a blue strip. Apply a thin layer of glue to the bottom of the coil and place it to the right of the coil applied in step 14.

**16**

Make an open coil using a navy strip. Apply a thin layer of glue to the bottom of the coil and place it inside the right-hand fin, with the end of the strip curving from the left upwards to the tip.

**17**

Slightly bend a piece of azure strip. Apply a thin layer of glue to the bottom of the strip and place it inside the same fin, extending from above the scroll to the tip of the fin.

**18**

Slightly bend a piece of blue strip. Apply a thin layer of glue to the bottom of the strip and place inside the fin to the right of the strip applied in step 17.

**19**

Make a coil using an azure strip. Apply a thin layer of glue to the bottom of the coil and place it inside the fin to the left of the step 16 coil, with the end of the strip curving up from the right and following the left side of the fin.

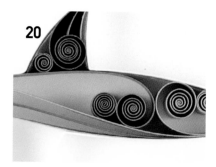

**20**

Make a coil using an azure strip. Apply a thin layer of glue to the bottom of the coil and place it in the shark's body to the left of the coil applied in step 13.

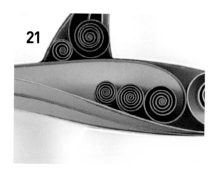

**21**

Make a smaller coil using an azure strip. Apply a thin layer of glue to the bottom of the coil and place it to the left of the coil applied in step 20.

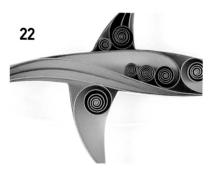

**22**

Make an open coil using a blue strip. Apply a thin layer of glue to the bottom of the coil. Place it inside the left-hand fin, with the end of the strip extending from above and down the left side to the fin's tip.

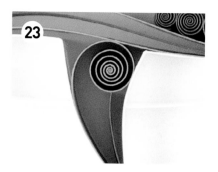

**23**

Slightly bend a piece of navy strip. Apply a thin layer of glue to the bottom of the strip and place it inside the same fin, extending from the bottom of the coil applied in step 22 to the fin's tip.

**24**

Slightly bend a piece of azure strip. Apply a thin layer of glue to the bottom of the strip and place it inside the same fin to the left of the strip applied in step 23.

**25**

Make a tight coil using a blue strip (see page 11). Apply a thin layer of glue to the bottom of the coil and place it inside the same fin to the left of the coil applied in step 22.

**26**

Slightly bend a piece of light blue strip. Apply a thin layer of glue to the bottom of the strip. Place it along the bottom edge of the shark's body between the fin and tail, leaving no gap between it and the cardstock.

**27**

Slightly bend a piece of light blue strip. Apply a thin layer of glue to the bottom of the strip and place it along the top of the belly section, leaving no gap between it and the cardstock.

**28**

Slightly bend another piece of light blue strip. Apply a thin layer of glue to the bottom of the strip and place it above the strip applied in step 26.

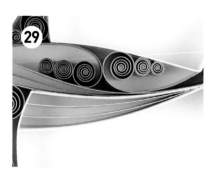

**29**

Slightly bend another piece of light blue strip. Apply a thin layer of glue to the bottom of the strip and place it above the strip applied in step 28.

**30**

Slightly bend another piece of light blue strip. Apply a thin layer of glue to the bottom of the strip. Place it along the bottom edge between the left-hand fin and the mouth, leaving no gap between it and the cardstock.

**31**

Slightly bend another piece of light blue strip. Apply a thin layer of glue to the bottom of the strip. Place it along the top edge between the left-hand fin and the mouth, leaving no gap between it and the cardstock.

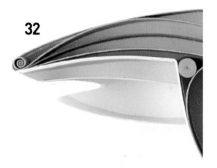

**32**

Slightly bend another piece of light blue strip. Apply a thin layer of glue to the bottom of the strip and place it as shown, starting just above the mouth and extending to the left-hand fin.

**33**

Slightly bend another piece of light blue strip. Apply a thin layer of glue to the bottom of the strip and place it as shown, starting just below the mouth and extending to the left-hand fin.

**34**

Make a small tight coil using a black strip.

**35**

Apply a thin layer of glue to the bottom of the coil and place it as shown near the nose and between the steps 10 and 11 strips.

# Cupcake

You need only two colours to create the illusion of icing swirling around this cupcake, and the cherry on top will complete the picture perfectly.

## materials

- Template on page 149
- Blank sheet of 90lb (250gsm) cardstock
- ⅜in (1cm) strips of 90lb (250gsm) cardstock
- 11 x ⅜in (28 x 1cm) red paper x 1
- 11 x ⅜in (28 x 1cm) cream paper x 2
- 11 x ⅜in (28 x 1cm) light pink paper x 2
- 11 x ⅜in (28 x 1cm) purple paper x 1
- 11 x ⅜in (5 x 1cm) black paper x 1

## tools

- Scissors
- Tweezers
- White glue
- Quilling tool (optional)

**1**

To create your base, place a sheet of blank cardstock under the template, then trace the outline onto it (see page 8). (Here, the outline has been darkened for clarity.)

**2**

Use strips of cardstock to prepare the outline of the cupcake (see page 8).

**3**

Make a C scroll using a red strip (see page 12). Apply a thin layer of glue to the bottom of the strip and place it inside the cherry, with the scrolls at the top and the largest one on the left-hand side.

**4**

Make a coil using a red strip (see page 10). Apply a thin layer of glue to the bottom of the strip and place it below the smaller coil in the C scroll applied in step 3.

**5**

Make an asymmetric scroll using a cream strip (see page 12). Apply a thin layer of glue to the bottom of the scroll and place it in the icing section below the cherry, with the end of the strip curving to the right.

**6**

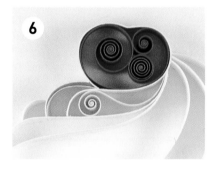

Slightly bend a short piece of light pink strip. Apply a thin layer of glue to the bottom of the strip and place it in the icing section to the left of the scroll applied in the previous step.

**7**

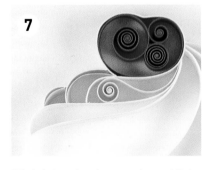

Slightly bend a shorter piece of light pink strip. Apply a thin layer of glue to the bottom of the strip and place it in the icing section to the left of the strip applied in the previous step.

**8**

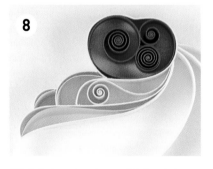

Slightly bend a piece of light pink strip. Apply a thin layer of glue to the bottom of the strip and place it in the icing section below the strips applied previously.

**9**

Make a bent drop shape using a light pink strip (see page 16). Apply a thin layer of glue to the bottom of the shape and place it in the large icing section below the strips applied previously.

**10**

Make an open coil using a cream strip (see page 11). Apply a thin layer of glue to the bottom of the coil and place it inside the bent drop shape, with the end of the strip curving from the bottom up to the right.

**11**

Make a smaller open coil using a cream strip. Apply a thin layer of glue to the bottom of the coil and place it to the right of the step 10 coil, with the long end of the strip extending to the right.

**12**

Slightly bend a piece of light pink strip. Apply a thin layer of glue to the bottom of the strip and place it in the icing section to the right of the shapes applied previously.

**13**

Slightly bend a piece of cream strip. Apply a thin layer of glue to the bottom of the strip and place it to the right of the strip applied in step 12.

**14**

Slightly bend a piece of light pink strip. Apply a thin layer of glue to the bottom of the strip and place it as in

the icing section to the right of the strip applied in step 13.

**15**

Slightly bend a piece of cream strip. Apply a thin layer of glue to the bottom of the strip and place it to the right of the light pink strip applied in step 14.

**16**

Slightly bend a shorter piece of light pink strip. Apply a thin layer of glue to the bottom of the strip and place it in the icing section to the right of the cream strip applied in step 15.

**17**

Slightly bend a short piece of cream strip. Apply a thin layer of glue to the bottom of the strip and place it in the icing section to the right of the light pink strip applied in step 16.

**18**

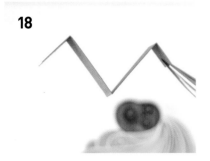

Make a zigzag shape using a purple strip (see page 14).

**19**

Apply a thin layer of glue to the bottom of the shape and place it across the bottom of the cupcake.

**20**

Make a V shape using a purple strip (see page 13). Apply a thin layer of glue to the bottom of the strip and place it centred above the zigzag shape applied in step 19, with the ends of the strip touching the icing.

**21**

Apply a thin layer of glue to the bottom of a short purple strip and place it to the left of the V shape, parallel to the left-hand end of the zigzag shape.

**22**

Apply a thin layer of glue to the bottom of another short purple strip and place it to the right of the V shape, parallel to the right-hand end of the zigzag shape.

**23**

Make an asymmetric V shape using a purple strip. Apply a thin layer of glue to the bottom of the strip and place it at the bottom left of the cupcake, parallel to the zigzag shape above it.

**24**

Make another asymmetric V shape using a purple strip. Apply a thin layer of glue to the bottom of the strip and place it at the bottom right of the cupcake, parallel to the zigzag shape above it.

**25**

Slightly bend a piece of black strip. Apply a thin layer of glue to the bottom of the strip and place it on top of the cherry at the top of the cupcake.

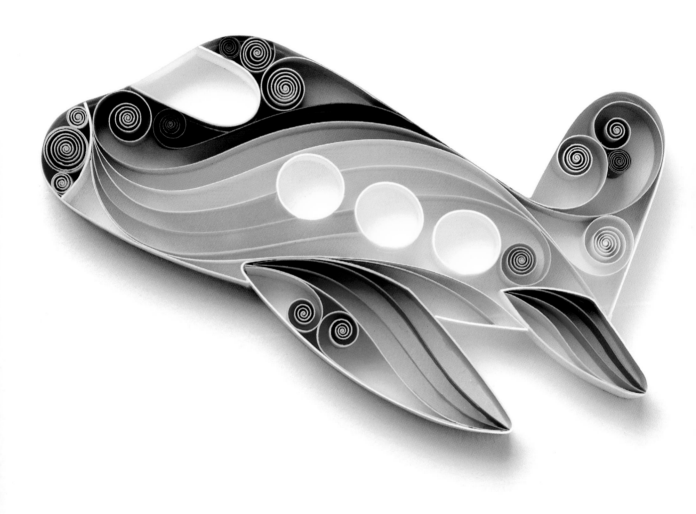

# Aeroplane

Wave shapes and coils suggest an aeroplane gliding through the air, but by using lots of different colours you can make this look even cuter.

## materials

- Template on page 148
- Blank sheet of 90lb (250gsm) cardstock
- ⅜in (1cm) strips of 90lb (250gsm) cardstock
- 11 x ⅜in (28 x 1cm) lavender paper x 1
- 11 x ⅜in (28 x 1cm) purple paper x 1
- 11 x ⅜in (28 x 1cm) lilac paper x 1
- 11 x ⅜in (28 x 1cm) light yellow paper x 2
- 11 x ⅜in (28 x 1cm) yellow paper x 1
- 11 x ⅜in (28 x 1cm) amber paper x 1
- 11 x ⅜in (28 x 1cm) azure paper x 1
- 11 x ⅜in (28 x 1cm) blue paper x 1
- 11 x ⅜in (28 x 1cm) mint paper x 2

## tools

- Scissors
- Tweezers
- White glue
- Quilling tool (optional)

**1**

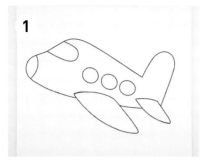

To create your base, place a sheet of blank cardstock under the template, then trace the outline onto it (see page 8). (Here, the outline has been darkened for clarity.)

**2**

Use strips of cardstock to prepare the outline of the aeroplane (see page 8).

**3**

Using a lavender strip, make a shape similar to a C scroll, but bend the middle section, as shown (see page 12).

**4**

Apply a thin layer of glue to the bottom of the scroll and place it across the plane with the scrolls curving upwards – one to the right of the plane's nose (on the left) and the other in the plane's tail.

**5**

Make an asymmetric scroll using a purple strip (see page 12). Apply a thin layer of glue to the bottom of the scroll. Place it between the previous scroll and the cockpit window, with the end of the strip extending from below to the right.

**6**

Make an open coil using a lilac strip (see page 11). Apply a thin layer of glue to the bottom of the coil and place it to the top right of the cockpit window, with the end of the strip extending from above to the right.

**7**

Make a coil using a lavender strip (see page 10). Apply a thin layer of glue to the bottom of the coil and place it above the cockpit window to the left of the coil applied in step 6.

**8**

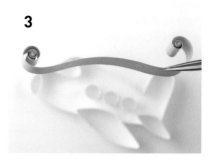

Make a smaller coil using a purple strip. Apply a thin layer of glue to the bottom of the coil and place it to the left of the coil applied in step 7.

Make an open coil using a lilac strip. Apply a thin layer of glue to the bottom of the coil and place it in the tail below the lavender scroll, with the end of the strip extending from the right and down to the left.

Make a smaller coil using a purple strip. Apply a thin layer of glue to the bottom of the coil and place it in the tail, as shown.

**11**

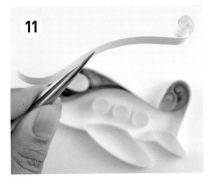

**12**

**13**

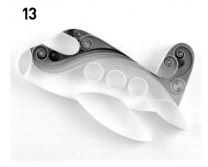

Make an asymmetric scroll shape using a light yellow strip, bending the end of the strip as shown.

Apply a thin layer of glue to the bottom of the scroll and place it below the C scroll applied in step 4, with the scroll on the right and the end of the strip extending from above, from right to left.

Slightly bend a yellow strip. Apply a thin layer of glue to the bottom of the strip and place it between the cabin window on the left and the small wing, following the curve of the strips above.

**14**

**15**

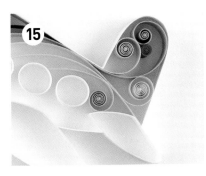

**16**

Slightly bend another yellow strip. Apply a thin layer of glue to the bottom of the strip and place it as shown from the nose to the cabin window on the left, following the curve of the strips above.

Make an open coil using an amber strip. Apply a thin layer of glue to the bottom of the coil. Place it with the coil to the right of the three windows, with the end of the strip curving from the right and up towards the centre window.

Slightly bend an amber strip. Apply a thin layer of glue to the bottom of the strip and place it between the left-hand porthole window and the nose on the left, following the curve of the strips above.

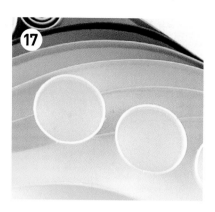

**17**

Cut a tiny strip of amber paper. Apply a thin layer of glue to the bottom of the strip and place it as shown between the left and middle cabin windows.

**18**

Slightly bend a yellow strip. Apply a thin layer of glue to the bottom of the strip and place it below the strip applied in step 16, extending from the nose to the cabin window in the centre.

**19**

Make a wave shape using a light yellow strip (see page 13). Apply a thin layer of glue to the bottom of the shape and place it below the step 18 strip, extending from the nose to the small wing.

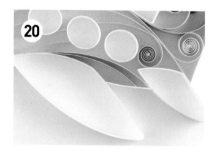

**20**

Slightly bend a lavender strip. Apply a thin layer of glue to the bottom of the strip and place it in the space between the two wings, below the step 19 strip.

**21**

Make a smaller wave shape using an azure strip. Apply a thin layer of glue to the bottom of the shape and place it in the small wing, on the right-hand side.

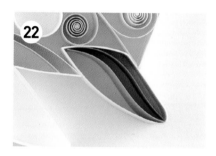

**22**

Make a smaller wave shape using a blue strip. Apply a thin layer of glue to the bottom of the shape and place it in the small wing, to the left of the shape applied in step 21.

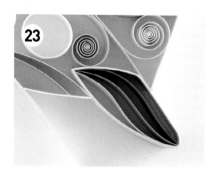

**23**

Make another smaller wave shape using a mint strip. Apply a thin layer of glue to the bottom of the shape and place it in the small wing, to the left of the shape applied in step 22.

**24**

Make a wave shape using an azure strip. Apply a thin layer of glue to the bottom of the shape and place it in the large wing, on the right-hand side.

**25**

Make a wave shape using a blue strip. Apply a thin layer of glue to the bottom of the shape and place it in the large wing, to the left of the shape applied in step 24.

**26**

Make a wave shape using a mint strip. Apply a thin layer of glue to the bottom of the shape and place it in the large wing, to the left of the shape applied in step 25.

**27**

Make an open coil using a mint strip. Apply a thin layer of glue to the bottom of the coil and place it in the bottom left of the large wing, with the end of the strip curving from the left downwards.

**28**

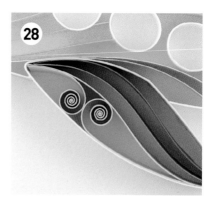

Make another open coil using a mint strip. Apply a thin layer of glue to the bottom of the coil and place it in the top left of the large wing, with the end of the strip curving from the right and up to the left.

**29**

Make a coil using a mint strip. Apply a thin layer of glue to the bottom of the coil and place it centred in the nose, as shown.

**30**

Make a smaller coil using a mint strip. Apply a thin layer of glue to the bottom of the coil and place it in the nose, above the coil applied in step 29.

**31**

Make another smaller coil using a mint strip. Apply a thin layer of glue to the bottom of the coil and place it in the nose below the coil applied in step 29.

# Scooter

With its wheels, saddle and headlight, here's a scooter any child would be delighted to find hanging in a bedroom – and it's a perfect gift for a scooter enthusiast.

## materials

- Template on page 146

- Blank sheet of 90lb (250gsm) cardstock

- ⅜in (1cm) strips of 90lb (250gsm) cardstock

- 11 x ⅜in (28 x 1cm) grey paper x 2

- 11 x ⅜in (28 x 1cm) black paper x 12

- 11 x ⅜in (28 x 1cm) navy paper x 1

- 11 x ⅜in (28 x 1cm) azure paper x 1

- 11 x ⅜in (28 x 1cm) blue paper x 1

- 11 x ⅜in (28 x 1cm) light blue paper x 2

- 11 x ⅜in (28 x 1cm) light green paper x 1

- 11 x ⅜in (28 x 1cm) mint paper x 1

- 2 x ⅜in (5 x 1cm) red paper x 1

- 2 x ⅜in (5 x 1cm) yellow paper x 1

## tools

- Scissors

- Tweezers

- White glue

- Quilling tool (optional)

**1**

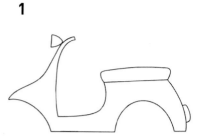

To create your base, place a sheet of blank cardstock under the template, then trace the outline onto it (see page 8). (Here, the outline has been darkened for clarity.)

**2**

Use strips of cardstock to prepare the outline of the scooter (see page 8).

**3**

Make a semi-tight coil using a grey strip (see page 11). Cover it using five black strips to create a wheel (see page 11). Repeat to make two wheels.

**4**

One at a time, apply a thin layer of glue to the bottom of the wheels and place them below the outline of the scooter.

**5**

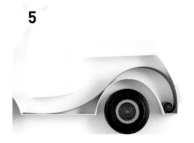

Make an asymmetric scroll using a navy strip (see page 12). Apply a thin layer of glue to the bottom and place it inside the outline over the rear wheel, with the end of the strip curving up to the bottom left.

**6**

Make a wave shape using an azure strip (see page 13).

**7**

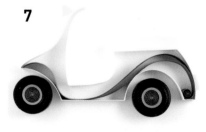

Apply a thin layer of glue to the bottom of the shape and place it above the scroll shape, extending all the way across the scooter from one end to the other.

**8**

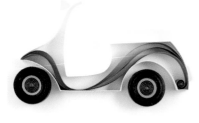

Make another wave shape using a blue strip. Apply a thin layer of glue to the bottom and place it above the shape applied in step 7, and touching it along the bottom edge.

**9**

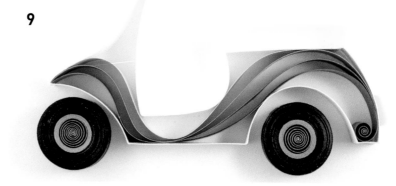

Make another wave shape using a light blue strip. Apply a thin layer of glue to the bottom of the shape and place it above the shape applied in step 8, again touching it along the bottom edge.

**10**

Make an open coil using a navy strip (see page 11). Apply a thin layer of glue to the bottom of the coil. Place it below the step 5 shape, with the end of the strip curving up and left.

**11**

Make a smaller open coil using a light green strip. Apply a thin layer of glue to the bottom of the coil and place it in the top left section just below the seat, with the end of the strip curving up and right.

**12**

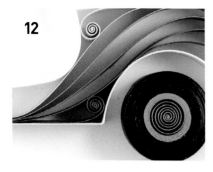

Make an open coil using a navy strip. Apply a thin layer of glue to the bottom of the coil and place it to the left of the rear wheel, with the end of the strip curving down and left.

**13**

Make a coil using a mint strip (see page 10). Apply a thin layer of glue to the bottom of the coil and place it centred in the bottom area between the two wheels.

**14**

Make a smaller coil using a light green strip. Apply a thin layer of glue to the bottom of the coil and place it to the right of the coil applied in step 13.

**15**

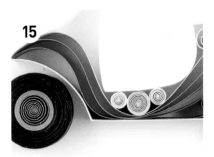

Make another smaller coil using a light green strip. Apply a thin layer of glue to the bottom of the coil and place it to the left of the step 13 coil.

**16**

Make an asymmetric scroll using a light blue strip. Apply a thin layer of glue to the bottom of the scroll.

Place it in the front handlebar area of the scooter, with the end of the strip curving up from the right.

**17**

Make a smaller open coil using a light green strip. Apply a thin layer of glue to the bottom of the coil. Place it in the handlebar area to the left of the step 16 scroll, with the end of the strip curving up from the left.

**18**

Make a coil using a blue strip. Apply a thin layer of glue to the bottom of the coil and place it in the front side of the scooter, below the scroll applied in step 16.

**19**

Make a smaller coil using an azure strip. Apply a thin layer of glue to the bottom of the coil and place it below the coil applied in step 18.

**20**

Make a very small coil using a navy strip. Apply a thin layer of glue to the bottom of the coil and place it below the coil applied in step 19.

**21**

Make another small coil using a light blue strip. Apply a thin layer of glue to the bottom of the coil and place it to the left of the step 16 scroll.

**22**

Make a coil using a black strip. Apply a thin layer of glue to the bottom of the coil and place it in the left-hand corner of the seat.

**23**

Make five more coils using black strips. One at a time, apply a thin layer of glue to the bottom of the

coils and place them next to each other to fill the seat.

**24**

Make a marquise shape using a red strip (see page 15). Apply a thin layer of glue to the bottom of the shape and place it in the tail light.

**25**

Make a marquise shape using a yellow strip. Apply a thin layer of glue to the bottom of the shape and

place it inside the headlight to the left of the handlebar.

**26**

Make a smaller coil using a blue strip. Apply a thin layer of glue to the bottom of the coil and place it inside the headlight, to the right of the marquise shape.

**27**

Make a smaller marquise shape using a black strip. Apply a thin layer of glue to the bottom of the

shape and place it in the top of the handlebar to make the brake.

# Bird

To create this bird you will be using different modern quilling shapes – bent drop shapes are perfect for creating a sense of movement in the wings.

## materials

- Template on page 149
- Blank sheet of 90lb (250gsm) cardstock
- ⅜in (1cm) strips of 90lb (250gsm) cardstock
- 11 x ⅜in (28 x 1cm) green paper x 4
- 11 x ⅜in (28 x 1cm) lime paper x 3
- 11 x ⅜in (28 x 1cm) emerald paper x 2
- 11 x ⅜in (28 x 1cm) seaweed paper x 1
- ⅜ x ⅜in (1 x 1cm) yellow paper
- ⅜ x ⅜in (1 x 1cm) black paper

## tools

- Scissors
- Tweezers
- White glue
- Quilling tool (optional)

**1**

To create your base, place a sheet of blank cardstock under the template, then trace the outline onto it (see page 8). (Here, the outline has been darkened for clarity.)

**2**

Use strips of cardstock to prepare the outline of the bird (see page 8).

**3**

Make an asymmetric scroll using a green strip (see page 12). Apply a thin layer of glue to the bottom of the scroll. Place it with the scroll in the bird's head and the end of the strip curving from below right to the tip of the tail at the left.

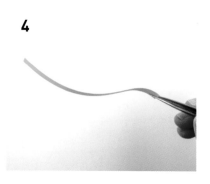

**4**

Using a lime strip, make the shape shown in the image.

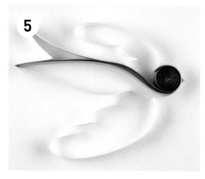

**5**

Apply a thin layer of glue to the bottom of the strip and place it below the asymmetric scroll, following its curve.

**6**

Slightly bend a green strip. Apply a thin layer of glue to the bottom of the strip and place it below the strip applied in step 5.

**7**

Slightly bend an emerald strip. Apply a thin layer of glue to the bottom of the strip and place it below the strip applied in step 6.

**8**

Slightly bend a seaweed strip. Apply a thin layer of glue to the bottom of the strip and place it under the strip applied in step 7, along the top of the bottom wing.

**9**

Make an open coil using an emerald strip (see page 11). Apply a thin layer of glue to the bottom of the coil and place it below the strip applied in step 8, with the end curving from below to the right.

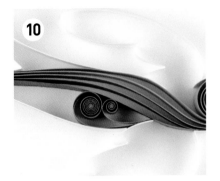

**10**

Make a smaller open coil using an emerald strip. Apply a thin layer of glue to the bottom of the coil. Place it to the right of the coil applied in step 9, with the end of the strip curving from below to the right.

**11**

Make an open coil using a lime strip. Apply a thin layer of glue to the bottom of the coil and place it to the left of the larger coil, with the end of the strip curving up and to the tail at the left.

**12**

Make a smaller open coil using a lime strip. Apply a thin layer of glue to the bottom of the coil and place it to the left side of the step 11 coil, with the end of the strip also curving up and to the left.

**13**

Slightly bend a green strip. Apply a thin layer of glue to the bottom of the strip and place it in the upper section of the tail, following the top edge of the outline.

**14**

Slightly bend a lime strip. Apply a thin layer of glue to the bottom of the strip and place it in the top tail section, below the step 13 strip.

**15**

Make a bent drop shape using an emerald strip (see page 16).

**16**

Apply a thin layer of glue to the bottom of the shape and place it in the right wing, with the loop on the left and the ends of the strip running up to the bird's head.

**17**

Make a narrower bent drop shape using a green strip. Apply a thin layer of glue to the bottom of the shape and place it inside the previous bent drop shape.

**18**

Make a narrower bent drop shape using a lime strip. Apply a thin layer of glue to the bottom of the shape and place it inside the step 17 bent drop shape.

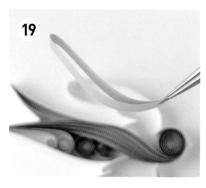

**19** Make a narrower bent drop shape using a lime strip for the next wing section. Note that the sections – and strips – get progressively smaller. Make another narrower bent drop shape using a green strip.

**20** One at a time, apply a thin layer of glue to the bottom of the bent drop shapes. First place the lime shape in the wing section above the previous one, with the loop on the left, then place the green shape inside it.

**21** Make a bent drop shape using a green strip. Apply a thin layer of glue to the bottom of the shape and place it in the wing section above the one filled in step 20, with a slight gap between them.

**22** Make a narrower bent drop shape using a lime strip. Apply a thin layer of glue to the bottom of the shape and place it inside the step 21 bent drop shape.

**23** Make a very small bent drop shape using a seaweed strip. Apply a thin layer of glue to the bottom of the shape and place it in the gap between the second and third sections of the bottom wing.

**24** Make a narrower bent drop shape using a lime strip. Apply a thin layer of glue to the bottom of the shape. Place it in the top section of the bottom wing, with the loop on the left and the ends running up to the right.

**25** Make a very small bent drop shape using a green strip. Apply a thin layer of glue to the bottom of the shape and place it inside the shape applied in step 24.

**26** Make a bent drop shape using a green strip. Apply a thin layer of glue to the bottom and place it in the top section of the left wing as shown, with the loop on the left and the ends running down to the right.

**27** Make a narrower bent drop shape using a lime strip. Apply a thin layer of glue to the bottom of the shape and place it inside the step 26 bent drop shape.

**28**

Make a bent drop shape using an emerald strip. Apply a thin layer of glue to the bottom of the shape and place it in the section of the wing below the bent drop shapes in steps 26–27.

**29**

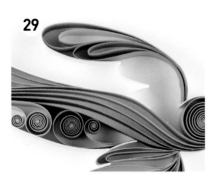

Make a narrower bent drop shape using a green strip. Apply a thin layer of glue to the bottom of the shape and place it inside the bent drop shape applied in step 28.

**30**

Make a bent drop shape using a lime strip. Apply a thin layer of glue to the bottom of the shape and place it as shown in the section of the wing below the bent drop shapes in steps 28–29.

**31**

Make a narrower bent drop shape using an emerald strip. Apply a thin layer of glue to the bottom of the shape and place it inside the bent drop shape applied in step 30.

**32**

Make an open coil using a green strip. Apply a thin layer of glue to the bottom of the coil and place it in the bottom section of the top wing, with the end of the strip curving down from right to left.

**33**

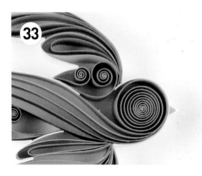

Make a smaller open coil using a green strip. Apply a thin layer of glue to the bottom of the coil and place it to the left of the step 32 open coil, with the end of the strip extending down from right to left.

**34**

Make a small V shape using a yellow strip (see page 13).

**35**

Cut a small rectangle shape using a black strip to represent the bird's eye.

**36**

Apply a thin layer of glue to the bottom of the yellow V shape and place it inside the bird's beak. Apply a thin layer of glue to the back of the black rectangle and place it on the head.

# Ampersand

Pink, lilac and shades of yellow forming coils, scrolls and marquises create a cheerful ampersand – a symbol that has been around since Roman times.

## materials

- Template on page 149
- Blank sheet of 90lb (250gsm) cardstock
- ⅜in (1cm) strips of 90lb (250gsm) cardstock
- 11 x ⅜in (28 x 1cm) lavender paper x 1
- 11 x ⅜in (28 x 1cm) light pink paper x 1
- 11 x ⅜in (28 x 1cm) cream paper x 1
- 11 x ⅜in (28 x 1cm) light yellow paper x 2
- 11 x ⅜in (28 x 1cm) yellow paper x 2
- 11 x ⅜in (28 x 1cm) amber paper x 1
- 11 x ⅜in (28 x 1cm) lilac paper x 1
- 11 x ⅜in (28 x 1cm) bubblegum pink paper x 2

## tools

- Scissors
- Tweezers
- White glue
- Quilling tool (optional)

**1**

To create your base, place a sheet of blank cardstock under the template, then trace the outline onto it (see page 8). (Here, the outline has been darkened for clarity.)

**2**

Use strips of cardstock to prepare the outline of the ampersand (see page 8).

**3**

Make an asymmetric scroll using a lavender strip (see page 12). Apply a thin layer of glue to the bottom of the scroll. Place it as shown, with the end of the strip curving down from the right to the bottom right tip.

**4**

Slightly bend a light pink strip. Apply a thin layer of glue to the bottom of the strip and place it to the right of the strip applied in step 3.

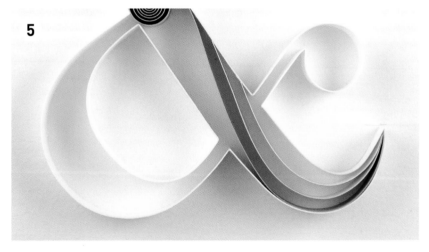

**5**

Slightly bend a shorter piece of a cream strip. Apply a thin layer of glue to the bottom of the strip and place it to the right of the strip applied in step 4.

**6**

Make an S scroll using a light yellow strip (see page 12). Apply a thin layer of glue to the bottom of the scroll. Place it in the section above the strips applied in steps 3–5.

**7**

Make a C shape using a yellow strip (see page 12).

**8**

Apply a thin layer of glue to the bottom of the shape and place it curving around the right-hand side of the large end of the scroll applied in step 7.

**9**

Make a C shape using an amber strip. Apply a thin layer of glue to the bottom of the shape and place it curving around the right-hand side of the C shape applied in step 8, with no gap between it and the outline.

**10**

Make an open coil using a lilac strip (see page 11). Apply a thin layer of glue to the bottom of the coil. Place it below the step 3 scroll, with the end of the strip curving left and down along the edge.

**11**

Make a tight coil using a cream strip (see page 11) and cover it using a lilac strip (see page 11). Apply a thin layer of glue to the bottom of the coil and place it below the big end of the coil applied in step 10.

**12**

Make a small coil using a cream strip (see page 10). Apply a thin layer of glue to the bottom of the coil and place it below the coil applied in step 11.

**13**

Following the method for making an S scroll, make the shape shown here using a bubblegum pink strip.

**14**

Apply a thin layer of glue to the bottom of the shape and place it above the step 3 scroll with the end of the strip curving up and around inside the top loop.

**15**

Slightly bend an amber strip. Apply a thin layer of glue to the bottom of the strip and place it starting at the large end of the step 14 scroll, on the top left side, with no gap between it and the outline.

**16**

Slightly bend a yellow strip. Apply a thin layer of glue to the bottom of the strip and place it to the right of the strip applied in step 15.

**17**

Slightly bend a shorter light yellow strip. Apply a thin layer of glue to the bottom of the strip and place it to the right of the strip applied in step 16.

**18**

Following the method for making an S scroll, make the shape shown here using a light pink strip.

**19**

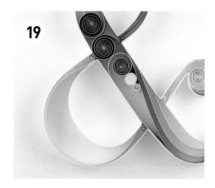

Apply a thin layer of glue to the bottom of the shape and place it in the bottom loop of the ampersand.

**20**

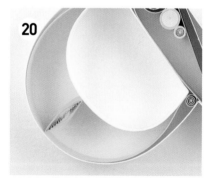

Make a marquise shape using an amber strip (see page 15). Apply a thin layer of glue to the bottom of the shape and place it centred in the bottom loop.

**21**

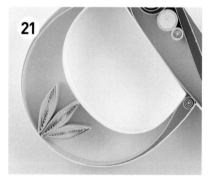

Make two more marquise shapes using a yellow strip. One at a time, apply a thin layer of glue to the bottom of the shapes and place them on either side of the marquise shape applied in step 20.

**22**

Make two more marquise shapes using a light yellow strip. Apply a thin layer of glue to the bottom of the shapes and place them on either side of the marquise shapes applied in step 21.

**23**

Slightly bend a shorter bubblegum pink strip. Apply a thin layer of glue to the bottom of the strip and place it above the marquise shapes, curving up from left to right.

**24**

Slightly bend another shorter bubblegum pink strip. Apply a thin layer of glue to the bottom of the strip and place it as shown, curving from the bottom right of the marquise shapes up to the right.

**25**

Make two asymmetric scrolls using bubblegum pink strips. One at a time, apply glue to the bottom of the scrolls and place them next to the marquise shapes, with the ends of the strips curving up and away from them.

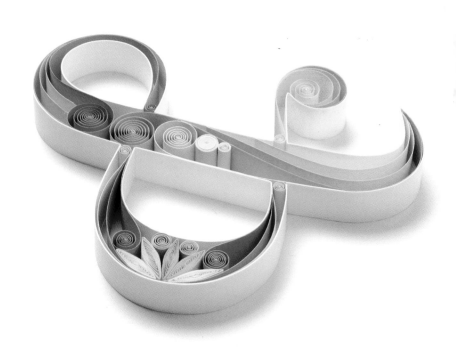

**26**

Make two coils using a lavender strip. One at a time, apply a thin layer of glue to the bottom of the coils and place them on either side of the central marquise shape.

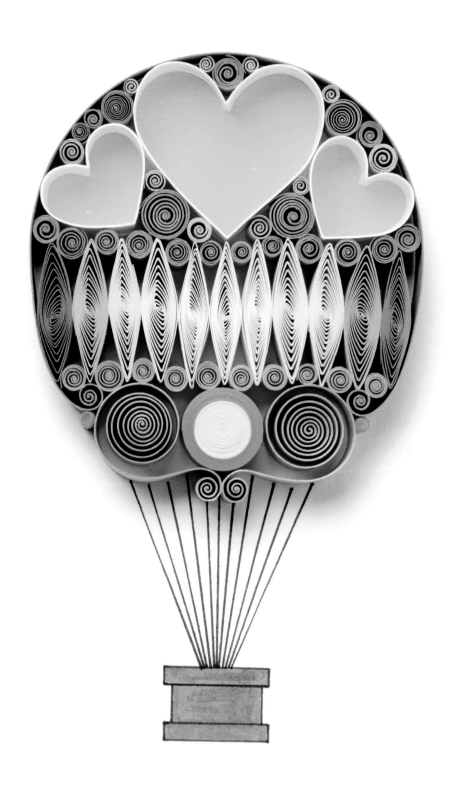

# Hot-air balloon

The coils, marquise shapes and hearts in this almost symmetrical hot-air balloon spark a sense of joy that will make you wish you were flying in it.

## materials

- Template on page 150
- Blank sheet of 90lb (250gsm) cardstock
- 11 x ⅜in (28 x 1cm) strips of 90lb (250gsm) cardstock
- 3¼ x 1¼in (8 x 4cm) amber paper x 1
- 11 x ⅜in (28 x 1cm) lilac paper x 3
- 11 x ⅜in (28 x 1cm) light yellow paper x 4
- 11 x ⅜in (28 x 1cm) pink paper x 4
- 11 x ⅜in (28 x 1cm) cream paper x 1
- 11 x ⅜in (28 x 1cm) light green paper x 2
- 11 x ⅜in (28 x 1cm) mint paper x 2
- 11 x ⅜in (28 x 1cm) seafoam paper x 2
- 11 x ⅜in (28 x 1cm) emerald paper x 2
- 11 x ⅜in (28 x 1cm) violet paper x 2
- 11 x ⅜in (28 x 1cm) purple paper x 1
- 11 x ⅜in (28 x 1cm) orange paper x 2

## tools

- Scissors
- Tweezers
- White glue
- Quilling tool (optional)
- Circular ruler
- Black and brown marker pens

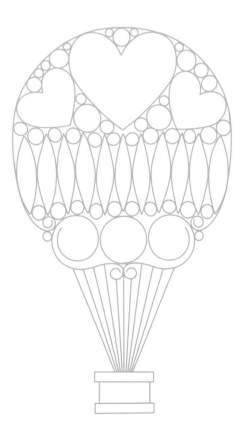

**1**

Using the template, draw the basket and ropes of the hot-air balloon on a sheet of blank cardstock and colour in the basket.

**2**

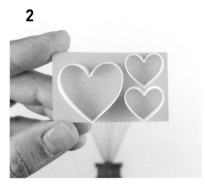

Using the template, use strips of cardstock to prepare the outlines of one big and two small hearts (see page 8). Apply a layer of glue to the bottom of the shapes and place them on a piece of amber paper.

**3**

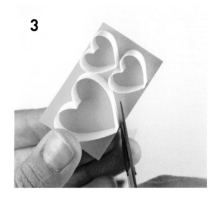

After the glue has dried, cut around the hearts, separating the shapes.

**4**

Trim the paper base right up to the white edges so that the amber colour is seen only inside the hearts. Do not glue the hearts in place yet (they will be glued down in a later step).

**5**

Make two S scrolls using lilac strips (see page 12). Apply a thin layer of glue to the bottom of both S scrolls and place them above the ropes, with the smaller ends meeting at the centre.

**6**

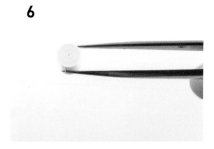

Make a tight coil using two light yellow strips (see page 11).

**7**

Cover the yellow coil using two pink strips (see page 11).

**8**

Apply glue to the bottom of the yellow and pink coil and place it centred between the two S scrolls.

**9**

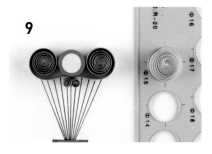

Create a coil using a cream strip (see page 10). Place the coil in a ⅝in (1.5cm)-diameter circle in the circular ruler and allow it to expand to fit (see page 11).

**10**

Make it into a marquise shape by squeezing two edges together (see page 15).

**11**

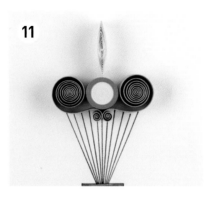

Apply a thin layer of glue to the bottom of the marquise shape and place it centred above the pink and yellow coil.

**12**

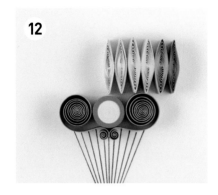

Using a light yellow strip, make a marquise shape. Apply a layer of glue to the bottom of the shape and place it to the right of the first marquise shape. Repeat using light green, mint, seafoam and emerald strips, respectively.

**13**

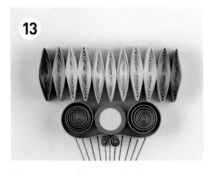

Repeat step 12 to make five more marquise shapes, but glue them to the left side of the first marquise, reversing the order of the colours from right to left.

**14**

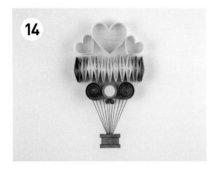

Apply glue to the bottom of the previously prepared heart shapes and place them over the marquise shapes, with the largest heart in the centre.

**15**

Make a symmetrical C scroll using a violet strip (see page 12).

**16**

Apply a thin layer of glue to the bottom of the scroll and place it around the marquise shapes and hearts to form the top of the hot-air balloon.

**17**

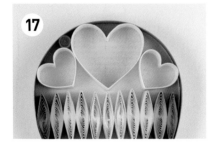

Make a coil using a purple strip. Apply a thin layer of glue to the bottom of the coil and place it above the smaller left-hand heart and to the left of the large heart.

**18**

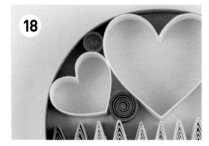

Make a coil using a violet strip. Apply a thin layer of glue to the bottom of the coil and place it between the left-hand and large hearts, just above the marquise shapes.

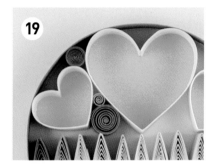

**19**

Make a small coil using a lilac strip. Apply a thin layer of glue to the bottom of the coil and place it between the first two hearts, above the coil applied in step 18.

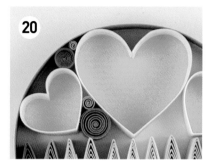

**20**

Make a smaller coil using a lilac strip. Apply a thin layer of glue to the bottom of the coil and place it to the right of the purple coil applied in step 17.

**21**

Make a small coil using a violet strip. Apply a thin layer of glue to the bottom of the coil and place it to the left of the purple coil applied in step 17.

**22**

Make a small coil using a purple strip. Apply a thin layer of glue to the bottom of the coil and place it to the left of the violet coil applied in step 21.

**23**

Make a small coil using a lilac strip. Apply a thin layer of glue to the bottom of the coil and place it to the left of the purple coil applied in step 22.

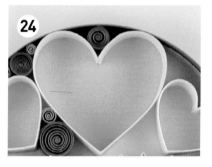

**24**

Make a coil using a violet strip. Apply a thin layer of glue to the bottom of the coil and place it at the top, centred over the large heart.

**25**

Make a small coil using a lilac strip. Apply a thin layer of glue to the bottom of the coil and place it to the left of the violet coil applied in step 24.

**26**

Make four coils using pink strips. One at a time, apply a thin layer of glue to the bottom of the coils and place them in the spaces between the top points of marquise shapes on the left-hand side of the balloon.

**27**

Make a coil using a violet strip. Apply a thin layer of glue to the bottom of the coil and place it to the left of the pink coils.

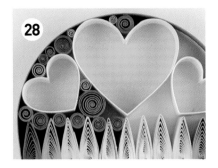

**28**

Make a coil using a pink strip. Apply a thin layer of glue to the bottom of the coil and place it to the right of the pink coils.

**29**

Make a coil using a lilac strip. Apply a thin layer of glue to the bottom of the coil and place it above the pink coil applied in step 28.

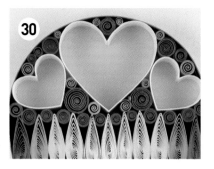

**30**

Repeat steps 17–23 and steps 25–29 to make the coils for the right-hand side of the balloon, placing them to form a mirror image of the left side.

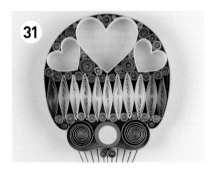

**31**

Make 10 coils using orange strips. One at a time, apply glue to the bottom of the coils and place them in the spaces between the bottom points of the marquise shapes.

**32**

Make two small tight coils using violet strips.

**33**

One at a time, apply a thin layer of glue to the bottom of the coils and place them to the left and right of the large ends of the lilac S scrolls as shown.

# Mandala

One of the more complex projects in this book, a mandala has repeating patterns to symbolize that everything in the universe is connected to each other.

## materials

- Template on page 148
- Blank sheet of 90lb (250gsm) cardstock
- ⅜in (1cm) strips of 90lb (250gsm) cardstock
- 11 x ⅜in (28 x 1cm) blue paper x 4
- 11 x ⅜in (28 x 1cm) teal paper x 9
- 11 x ⅜in (28 x 1cm) purple paper x 2
- 11 x ⅜in (28 x 1cm) pink paper x 1
- 11 x ⅜in (28 x 1cm) yellow paper x 1
- 11 x ⅜in (28 x 1cm) amber paper x 1
- 11 x ⅜in (28 x 1cm) lilac paper x 5
- 11 x ⅜in (28 x 1cm) lavender paper x 5
- 11 x ⅜in (28 x 1cm) violet paper x 1
- 11 x ⅜in (28 x 1cm) mint paper x 12
- 11 x ⅜in (28 x 1cm) light green paper x 3

## tools

- Scissors
- Tweezers
- White glue
- Quilling tool (optional)
- Circular ruler

**1**

To create your base, place a sheet of blank cardstock under the template, then trace the outline onto it (see page 8). (Here, the outline has been darkened for clarity.)

**2**

Use strips of cardstock to prepare the outline of the mandala (see page 8).

**3**

Make four diamond shapes using blue strips and four using teal strips (see page 15). For each diamond shape, use an 8¾in (22cm) strip to make the coil and let it expand to a ³⁄₈in (1cm)-diameter circle in the circular ruler.

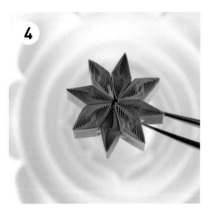

**4**

Glue all the diamonds together into an eight-pointed star shape, alternating the colours.

**5**

Apply a thin layer of glue to the bottom of the star shape and place it in the centre of the mandala.

**6**

Make eight coils from purple strips (see page 10). One at a time, apply a thin layer of glue to the bottom of the coils and place them in between the diamond shapes.

**7**

Make a circle using a pink strip. Apply a thin layer of glue to the bottom of the circle and place it around the exterior of the outline's central circle, without leaving a gap between them.

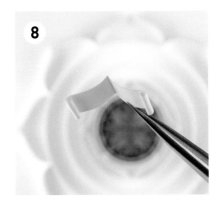

**8**

Follow the method for making a C scroll, adapting the shape as shown here to make four shapes using yellow strip (see page 12).

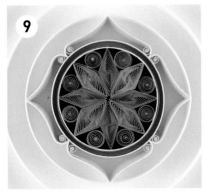

**9**

One at a time, apply a thin layer of glue to the bottom of the shapes and place them as shown in the next section, following the inside edge of the cardstock with the same shape.

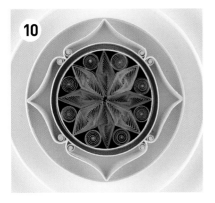

**10**

Make a circle using an amber strip. Apply a thin layer of glue to the bottom of the circle and place it inside the third circle from the centre, without leaving a gap between them.

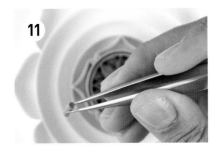

**11**

Make four smaller tight coils using a pink strip (see page 11).

**12**

One at a time, apply a thin layer of glue to the bottom of the coils and place them as shown inside the third circle and centred above the ends of where the step 9 shapes meet.

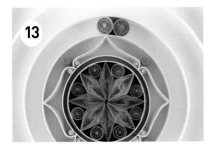

**13**

Make one coil from a lilac strip and one from a lavender strip. One at a time, apply a thin layer of glue to the bottom of the coils and place them together inside the fourth circle from the centre.

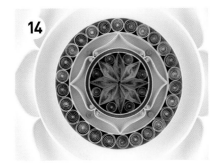

**14**

Make another 12 lilac coils and 12 lavender coils. One at a time, apply a thin layer of glue to the bottom of the coils and place them together inside the fourth circle, alternating the colours.

**15**

Make a circle using a violet strip. Apply a thin layer of glue to the bottom of the circle and place it on the outside edge of the fourth circle from the centre, without leaving a gap between them.

**16**

Make a circle using a teal strip. Apply a thin layer of glue to the bottom of the circle and place it on the inside edge of the fifth circle from the centre, without leaving a gap between them.

**17**

Following the adapted method used for the step 8 shapes, make four shapes using a teal strip.

**18**

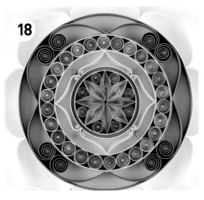

One at a time, apply a thin layer of glue to the bottom of the shapes and place them between the fourth and fifth circles from the centre.

**19**

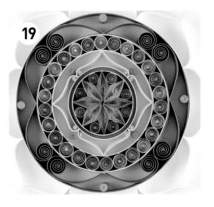

Make four tight coils using a blue strip. One at a time, apply a thin layer of glue to the bottom of the coils and place them centred above the shapes applied in step 18.

**20**

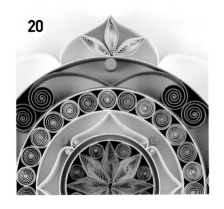

Make three marquise shapes using a 6in (15cm) mint strip and a ³⁄₈in (1cm)-diameter circle in a circle ruler (see page 15). One at a time, apply a thin layer of glue to the bottom of the shapes and place them in the top section of the mandala.

**21**

Make another 21 marquise shapes using mint strips. One at a time, apply a thin layer of glue to the bottom of the shapes and place them in the remaining exterior sections, with three per section.

**22**

Make two open coils using a light green strip (see page 11). Apply a thin layer of glue to the bottom of the coils and place them to each side of the top mint marquise, with the end of the strips curving towards it.

**23**

Make another 14 open coils using light green strips. One at a time, apply a thin layer of glue to the bottom of the coils and place them on each side of the remaining mint marquises.

# Llama

This festive South American llama is challenging, with a number of different shapes and colours, but it will take you to the next level in quilling art.

## materials

- Template on page 150
- Blank sheet of 90lb (250gsm) cardstock
- ⅜in (1cm) strips of 90lb (250gsm) cardstock
- 11 x ⅜in (28 x 1cm) bubblegum pink paper x 2
- 11 x ⅜in (28 x 1cm) lavender paper x 1
- 11 x ⅜in (28 x 1cm) lilac paper x 1
- 11 x ⅜in (28 x 1cm) cream paper x 1
- 11 x ⅜in (28 x 1cm) yellow paper x 1
- 11 x ⅜in (28 x 1cm) light yellow paper x 1
- 11 x ⅜in (28 x 1cm) light pink paper x 1
- 11 x ⅜in (28 x 1cm) light green paper x 1
- 11 x ⅜in (28 x 1cm) light blue paper x 1
- 11 x ⅜in 11 x ⅜in (28 x 1cm) blue paper x 1
- 11 x ⅜in (28 x 1cm) amber paper x 1
- 11 x ⅜in (28 x 1cm) emerald paper x 4
- 11 x ⅜in (28 x 1cm) pink paper x 1

## tools

- Scissors
- Tweezers
- White glue
- Quilling tool (optional)
- Circular ruler

**1**

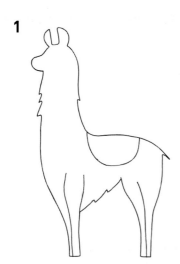

To create your base, place a sheet of blank cardstock under the template, then trace the outline onto it (see page 8). (Here, the outline has been darkened for clarity.)

**2**

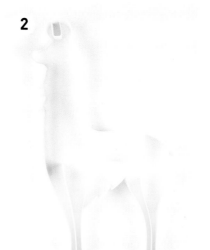

Use strips of cardstock to prepare the outline of the llama (see page 8).

**3**

Following the method for making an S scroll (see page 12), adapt it to make the shape shown here, using a bubblegum pink strip.

**4**

Apply a thin layer of glue to the bottom of the shape and place it in the llama's chest as shown, with the strip curving around in a circle and down the left side of the large coil to the right side of the small coil in the foreleg.

**5**

Make an asymmetric scroll using a lavender strip (see page 12). Apply a thin layer of glue to the bottom of the scroll. Place it in the llama's head, with the end of the strip curving from top right to bottom left.

**6**

Make an open coil using a lilac strip (see page 11). Apply a thin layer of glue to the bottom of the coil. Place it in the head, with the end of the strip wrapping around the top coil of the scroll applied in step 5.

**7**

Make a tight coil using a cream strip (see page 11). Apply a thin layer of glue to the bottom of the coil and place it between the two coils applied in steps 5 and 6.

**8**

Make an open coil using a yellow strip. Apply a thin layer of glue to the bottom of the coil and place it inside the ear on the left, with the end of the strip curving down the left side.

**9**

Make an open coil using a light yellow strip. Apply a thin layer of glue to the bottom of the coil and place it inside the other ear, with the end of the strip curving down the right side.

**10**

Make an open coil using a light pink strip. Apply a thin layer of glue to the bottom of the coil and place it in the llama's nose.

**11**

Make a wave shape using a light pink strip (see page 13). Apply a thin layer of glue to the bottom of the shape. Place it to the left of the end of the strip belonging to the shape applied in step 5.

**12**

Make a wave shape using a light yellow strip. Apply a thin layer of glue to the bottom of the shape and place it above the shape applied in step 11.

**13**

Make a wave shape using a yellow strip. Apply a thin layer of glue to the bottom of the shape and place it above the shape placed in step 12.

**14**

Make an asymmetric scroll using a lilac strip. Apply a thin layer of glue to the bottom of the scroll and place it in the top left area of the neck, with the end of the strip curving from above towards the right.

**15**

Make a wave shape using a lilac strip. Apply a thin layer of glue to the bottom of the shape and place it to the right of the wave shapes applied in steps 11–13.

**16**

Make an open coil using a light green strip. Apply a thin layer of glue to the bottom of the coil. Place it above the coil in the chest, with the end of the strip curving from above right and down to the left.

**17**

Make a coil using a light green strip (see page 10). Apply a thin layer of glue to the bottom of the coil and place it above the coil applied in step 16.

**18**

Make an open coil using a light pink strip. Apply a thin layer of glue to the bottom of the coil. Place it inside the circle in the chest, with the end of the strip curving from below left up the right-hand side of the circle.

**19**

Make a tight coil using a yellow strip. Apply a thin layer of glue to the bottom of the coil and place it to the left of the large coil inside the circle in the chest.

**20**

Make an asymmetric scroll using a lilac strip. Apply a thin layer of glue to the bottom of the scroll. Place in the front left leg, with the coil at the top and the end of the strip curving from the left down to the foot.

**21**

Make a tiny coil using a lilac strip. Apply a thin layer of glue to the bottom of the coil and place it in the front left foot, to the right of the previously placed strip.

**22**

Make a coil using a lavender strip. Apply a thin layer of glue to the bottom of the coil and place it in the top left corner of the left leg, above the lilac coil applied in step 20.

**23**

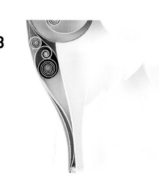

Slightly bend a piece of light pink strip. Apply a thin layer of glue to the bottom of the strip and place it inside the front left leg, to the left of the lilac strip applied in step 20.

**24**

Make an asymmetric scroll using a light blue strip. Apply a thin layer of glue to the bottom of the scroll. Place it inside the front right leg, with the end of the strip curving from above right down to the foot.

**25**

Make a tiny coil using a light blue strip. Apply a thin layer of glue to the bottom of the coil and place it inside the front right foot, to the left of the strip applied in step 24.

**26**

Slightly bend a piece of blue strip. Apply a thin layer of glue to the bottom of the strip and place it inside the front right leg, to the right of the strip applied in step 24.

**27**

Make a coil using a light blue strip. Apply a thin layer of glue to the bottom of the coil and place it under the scroll in the top area of the front right leg.

**28**

Make a tight coil using a cream strip and cover it using a lavender strip (see page 11). Apply a thin layer of glue to the bottom of the shape and place it to the top right of the front right leg.

**29**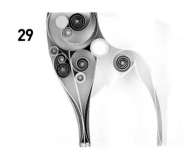

Make an asymmetric scroll using a light green strip. Apply a thin layer of glue to the bottom of the scroll and place it in the belly, with the end of the strip curving from above and down into the rear left leg.

**30**

Make an open coil using a cream strip. Apply a thin layer of glue to the bottom of the coil and place it to the left of the step 29 scroll, with the end of the strip curving up from the left to above right.

**31**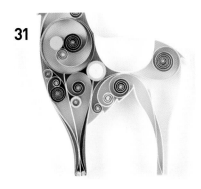

Make an S scroll using a light pink strip. Apply a thin layer of glue to the bottom of the scroll. Place it with the big coil in the rear, curving from below right to left, with the small coil in the left side of the belly.

**32**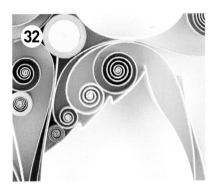

Make a small coil using a bubblegum pink strip. Apply a thin layer of glue to the bottom of the coil and place it in the bottom left corner of the belly.

**33**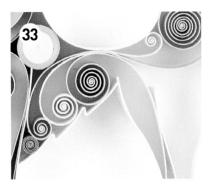

Make a small open coil using a cream strip. Apply a thin layer of glue to the bottom of the coil and place it below the saddle on the right side, with the end of the strip curving from below to the left.

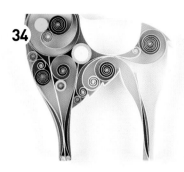

**34**

Cut a piece of light blue strip. Apply a thin layer of glue to the bottom of the strip and place it inside the left rear leg, to the right of the strip applied in step 29.

**35**

Make a tiny coil using a light green strip. Apply a thin layer of glue to the bottom of the coil and place it in the rear left foot, to the left of the previously placed strips.

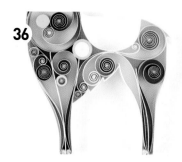

**36**

Make an asymmetric scroll using a bubblegum pink strip. Apply a thin layer of glue to the bottom of the scroll and place it inside the rear right leg, with the end of the strip curving down from the left.

**37**

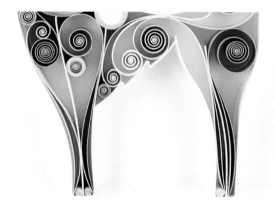

Slightly bend a piece of light pink strip. Apply a thin layer of glue to the bottom of the strip and place it

inside the rear right leg, to the left of the strip applied in step 36.

**38**

Make a tiny coil using a bubblegum pink strip. Apply a thin layer of glue to the bottom of the coil and place it in the rear right foot, to the right of the previously placed strips.

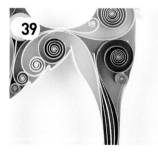

**39**

Make a coil using a bubblegum pink strip. Apply a thin layer of glue to the bottom of the coil and place it in the left rear leg, below the coil of the scroll applied in step 36.

**40**

Make a tight coil using a light blue strip. Apply a thin layer of glue to the bottom of the coil and place it between the two rear legs at the top.

**41**

Make a tight coil using an amber strip. Apply a thin layer of glue to the bottom of the coil and place it at the top right of the rear right leg, between the two large coils.

**42**

Make a marquise shape using an emerald strip (see page 15). (You can use a circular ruler here and in the next two steps.) Apply a thin layer of glue to the bottom of the shape. Place it in the centre of the saddle.

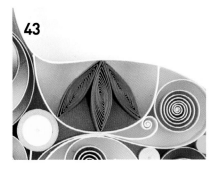

**43**

Make two slightly smaller marquise shapes using an emerald strip. One at a time, apply a thin layer of glue to the bottom of the shapes and place on either side of the first marquise, with points meeting at the top.

**44**

Make two more marquise shapes slightly smaller than those in step 43 using an emerald strip. One at a time, apply a thin layer of glue to the bottom of the shapes. Place them on either side of the other marquises.

**45**

Make two large, two medium and two small coils using a pink strip. Apply a thin layer of glue to the bottom of the coils. Place them in between the marquise shapes in order of size, as shown.

# Dragon

You will be using both repeating patterns and different quilling techniques to construct a blue dragon with flames shooting out of its mouth.

## materials

- Template on page 150

- Blank sheet of 90lb (250gsm) cardstock

- ⅜in (1cm) strips of 90lb (250gsm) cardstock

- 11 x ⅜in (28 x 1cm) azure paper x 6

- 11 x ⅜in (28 x 1cm) blue paper x 3

- 11 x ⅜in (28 x 1cm) navy paper x 2

- 11 x ⅜in (28 x 1cm) light blue paper x 6

- 11 x ⅜in (28 x 1cm) teal paper x 4

- 11 x ⅜in (28 x 1cm) red paper x 1

- 2 x ⅜in (5 x 1cm) yellow paper x 1

- 2 x ⅜in (5 x 1cm) amber paper x 1

## tools

- Scissors

- Tweezers

- White glue

- Quilling tool (optional)

**1**

To create your base, place a sheet of blank cardstock under the template, then trace the outline onto it (see page 8). (Here, the outline has been darkened for clarity.)

**2**

Use strips of cardstock to prepare the outline of the dragon (see page 8).

**3**

Make an asymmetric scroll using an azure strip (see page 12). Apply a thin layer of glue to the bottom of the scroll. Place it in the head, with the end of the strip curving from above to the left horn.

**4**

Make a small wave shape using an azure strip (see page 13). Apply a thin layer of glue to the bottom of the shape and place it above the dragon's eye.

**5**

Make a small open coil using an azure strip (see page 11). Apply a thin layer of glue to the bottom of the coil and place it to the left of the asymmetric scroll, with the end of the strip curving from right to left.

**6**

Following the methods for making an asymmetric scroll and a wave shape, make a shape as shown here, using an azure strip.

**7**

Apply a thin layer of glue to the bottom of the shape and place it along the bottom jaw, with the coil in the chin and the end of the strip curving up towards **the horn.**

**8**

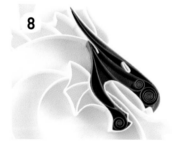

Slightly bend a short piece of azure strip. Apply a thin layer of glue to the bottom of the strip and place it in the jaw, above the shape applied in step 7.

**9**

Make a small wave shape using a blue strip. Apply a thin layer of glue to the bottom of the shape and place it in the right-hand horn.

**10**

Make a long asymmetric scroll using an azure strip. Apply a thin layer of glue to the bottom of the scroll. Place it in the neck, with the end curving from above the coil towards the left, down to the tip of the tail.

**11**

Make an open coil using a navy strip. Apply a thin layer of glue to the bottom of the coil and place it to the right of the coil in the neck, with the end of the strip curving from above to the left.

**12**

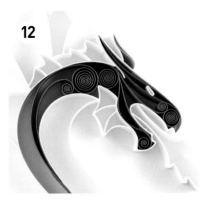

Make a smaller open coil using an azure strip. Apply a thin layer of glue to the bottom of the coil. Place it to the left of the step 10 scroll, with the end of the strip curving from above to the left.

**13**

Make an S shape using a blue strip (see page 12). Apply a thin layer of glue to the bottom of the shape and place it along the left edge of the body and tail, starting at the step 10 scroll, with no gap between it and the outline.

**14**

Make another S shape using a blue strip. Apply a thin layer of glue to the bottom of the shape and place it to the right of the S shape applied in step 13.

**15**

Make a C shape using a navy strip (see page 12). Apply a thin layer of glue to the bottom of the shape. Place it to the right of the step 10–14 shapes, in the lower section, with no gap between it and the outline.

**16**

Make the spade shape of the tail's tip using a navy strip. Apply a thin layer of glue to the bottom of the shape and place it inside the tip of the tail.

**17**

Following the method for making a wave shape (see page 13), adapt it to make the shape shown here, using an azure strip.

**18**

Glue the middle section of the shape together and let dry. Apply a thin layer of glue to the bottom of the shape and place it centred inside the tip of the tail.

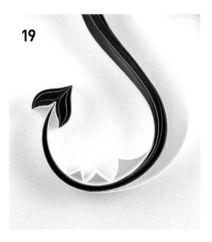

**19**

Make two small wave shapes using a blue strip. One at a time, apply a thin layer of glue to the bottom of the shapes and place them inside the tip of the tail on either side of the shape applied in step 18.

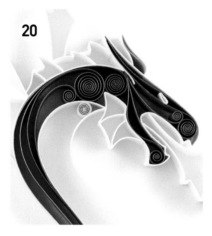

**20**

Make a small coil using a light blue strip (see page 10). Apply a thin layer of glue to the bottom of the coil and place it at the top of the front section of the neck.

**21**

Make twelve more coils in various sizes to fit in the front section of the body using light blue strips. One at a time, apply a thin layer of glue to the bottom of the coils and place them along the front of the body.

**22**

Make a coil using a teal strip. Apply a thin layer of glue to the bottom of the coil. Place it in the right-hand spine in the area above the curved section of the tail.

**23**

Make three smaller coils in various sizes using a teal strip. One at a time, apply a thin layer of glue to the bottom of the coils and place one to the left and two to the right of the coil applied in step 22.

**24**

Make another coil using a teal strip. Apply a thin layer of glue to the bottom of the coil and place it in the spine in the middle.

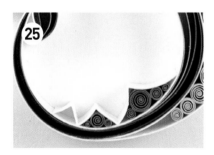

**25**

Make two smaller coils using a teal strip. One at a time, apply a thin layer of glue to the bottom of the coils and place them on each side of the coil applied in step 24.

**26**

Make another coil using a teal strip. Apply a thin layer of glue to the bottom of the coil and place it in the left-hand spine.

**27**

Make a smaller coil using a teal strip. Apply a thin layer of glue to the bottom of the coil and place it to the left of the coil applied in step 26.

**28**

Make a marquise shape using a teal strip (see page 15). Apply a thin layer of glue to the bottom of the shape and place it on the right-hand side of the frill above the dragon's neck (to the left of the horns).

**29**

Make a smaller marquise shape using an azure strip. Apply a thin layer of glue to the bottom of the shape and place it in the same section, to the left of the previous marquise shape.

**30**

Make one smaller teal and one bigger azure marquise shape. One at a time, apply a thin layer of glue to the bottom of the shapes and place them to the left of the shapes applied in steps 28–29.

**31**

Make one teal and one azure marquise shape. One at a time, apply a thin layer of glue to the bottom of the shapes and place them to the left of the shapes applied in step 30.

**32**

Make one teal and one azure marquise shape. One at a time, apply a thin layer of glue to the bottom of the shapes and place them to the left of the shapes applied in step 31.

**33**

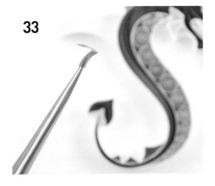

Following the methods for making a wave shape and a V shape (see page 13), adapt them to make the shape shown here, using an azure strip.

**34**

Apply a thin layer of glue to the bottom of the shape and place it in the top section of the frill below the dragon's jaw.

**35**

Slightly bend a short piece of blue strip. Apply a thin layer of glue to the bottom and place in the middle of the shape applied in step 34.

**36**

Repeat steps 33–35, placing the shapes in the middle section of the frill below the dragon's jaw.

**37**

Repeat steps 33–35 to finish the final section of the frill below the dragon's jaw.

**38**

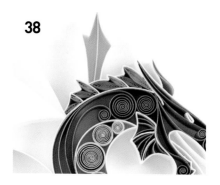

Cut a piece of light blue strip. Apply a thin layer of glue to the bottom of the strip and place it down the middle of the wing over the dragon's neck, visible above its frill.

**39**

Cut a shorter piece of blue strip. Apply a thin layer of glue to the bottom of the strip and place it to the right of the strip applied in step 38.

**40**

Slightly bend a short piece of azure strip. Apply a thin layer of glue to the bottom of the strip and place it to the right of the strip applied in step 39.

**41**

Repeat steps 39–40, placing the strips to the left of the light blue strip applied in step 38.

**42**

Slightly bend a piece of navy strip. Apply a thin layer of glue to the bottom of the strip and place it along the top edge of the right-hand wing, with no gap between it and the outline.

**43**

Slightly bend a piece of azure strip. Apply a thin layer of glue to the bottom of the strip and place it to the left of the strip applied in step 42.

**44**

Slightly bend a piece of blue strip. Apply a thin layer of glue to the bottom of the strip and place it to the left of the strip applied in step 43.

**45**

Slightly bend a piece of light blue strip. Apply a thin layer of glue to the bottom of the strip and place it to the left of the strip applied in step 44.

**46**

Cut a piece of light blue strip. Apply a thin layer of glue to the bottom of the strip and place it below the top edge of the middle section of the wing.

**47**

Working from top to bottom, one at a time slightly bend a blue, azure, navy, azure, blue and light blue strip. Apply a thin layer of glue to the bottom of each strip and place in the middle section of the wing.

**48**

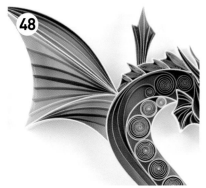

Working from top to bottom, one at a time slightly bend a light blue, blue, azure and navy strip. Apply a thin layer of glue to the bottom of each strip and place in the right-hand section of the wing.

**49**

Slightly bend a piece of red strip. Apply a thin layer of glue to the bottom of the strip and place it in the top section of the fire coming out of the dragon's mouth.

**50**

Cut a piece of yellow strip. Apply a thin layer of glue to the bottom of the strip and place it below the red strip in the dragon's fire.

**51**

Cut a piece of amber strip. Apply a thin layer of glue to the bottom of the strip and place it below the yellow strip in the dragon's fire.

**52**

Slightly bend a piece of red strip. Apply a thin layer of glue to the bottom of the strip and place it below the amber strip in the dragon's fire.

**53**

Slightly bend another piece of red strip. Apply a thin layer of glue to the bottom of the strip and place it below the strip applied in step 52.

**54**

Cut a very short piece of red strip. Apply a thin layer of glue to the bottom of the strip and place it inside the eye.

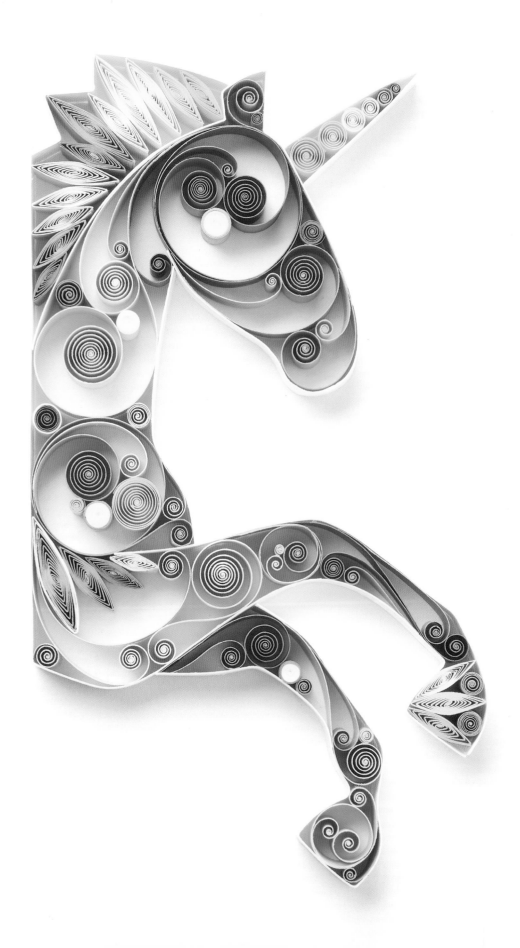

# Unicorn

With a rainbow of colours in coils and marquises making up its horn and mane, this galloping unicorn will transport you to a world of fairy tales.

## materials

- Template on page 148
- Blank sheet of 90lb (250gsm) cardstock
- ⅜in (1cm) strips of 90lb (250gsm) cardstock
- 11 x ⅜in (28 x 1cm) amber paper x 1
- 11 x ⅜in (28 x 1cm) yellow paper x 2
- 11 x ⅜in (28 x 1cm) light yellow paper x 2
- 11 x ⅜in (28 x 1cm) light pink paper x 1
- 11 x ⅜in (28 x 1cm) bubblegum pink paper x 3
- 11 x ⅜in (28 x 1cm) purple paper x 2
- 11 x ⅜in (28 x 1cm) cream paper x 3
- 11 x ⅜in (28 x 1cm) lavender paper x 1
- 11 x ⅜in (28 x 1cm) lilac paper x 1
- 11 x ⅜in (28 x 1cm) light blue paper x 1
- 11 x ⅜in (28 x 1cm) blue paper x 2
- 11 x ⅜in (28 x 1cm) teal paper x 2
- 11 x ⅜in (28 x 1cm) violet paper x 2
- 11 x ⅜in (28 x 1cm) mint paper x 2
- 11 x ⅜in (28 x 1cm) light green paper x 1

## tools

- Scissors
- Tweezers
- White glue
- Quilling tool (optional)
- Circular ruler

To create your base, place a sheet of blank cardstock under the template, then trace the outline onto it (see page 8). (Here, the outline has been darkened for clarity.)

Use strips of cardstock to prepare the outline of the unicorn (see page 8).

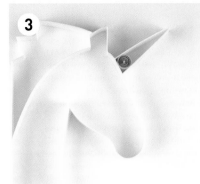

Make a coil using an amber strip (see page 10). Apply a thin layer of glue to the bottom of the coil and place it at the bottom of the horn.

From big to small, make five coils from a yellow, light yellow, light pink, bubblegum pink and purple strip. One at a time, apply a thin layer of glue to the bottom of the coils and place them in the horn.

Make a marquise shape using an amber strip (see page 15). Apply a thin layer of glue to the bottom of the marquise and place it in the top right part of the mane.

From small to big, make three marquise shapes with a yellow, light yellow and cream strip. One at a time, apply a thin layer of glue to the bottom of the shapes and place to the left of the first marquise.

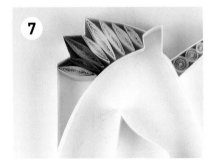

One at a time, make four marquise shapes of various sizes with a light pink, bubblegum pink, purple and lavender strip. Apply a thin layer of glue to the bottom and place to the left of the other marquises.

One at a time, make four more marquise shapes with a lilac, light blue, blue and teal strip. Apply a thin layer of glue to the bottom of the shapes and place them to the left of the previous marquises.

Make a C scroll, adapting the shape as shown here, using a violet strip (see page 12).

**10**

Apply a thin layer of glue to the bottom of the shape. Place it in the unicorn's head, with the strip curving in a circle around the larger coil and from above down the left, with the small coil in the neck.

**11**

Make an open coil using a purple strip (see page 11). Apply a thin layer of glue to the bottom of the coil. Place it below the step 10 shape, with the end of the strip curving from below to the left.

**12**

Make an open coil using a bubblegum pink strip (see page 11). Apply a thin layer of glue to the bottom of the coil. Place it below the step 11 shape, with the end of the strip curving from the left, along the edge of the head and up the right.

**13**

Make a smaller open coil using an amber strip. Apply a thin layer of glue to the bottom of the coil and place it to the right of the step 12 coil, with the end of the strip curving from below left and up to the right.

**14**

Make another smaller open coil using a lavender strip. Apply a thin layer of glue to the bottom of the coil. Place it to the left of the step 11 coil, with the end of the strip curving from below, from right to left.

**15**

Make a coil using a teal strip. Apply a thin layer of glue to the bottom of the coil and place it on the right-hand side of the head, between the steps 10 and 11 shapes.

**16**

Make an open coil using a teal strip. Apply a thin layer of glue to the bottom of the coil. Place it to the left of the step 10 coil, with the end of the strip curving from above left, following the purple strip.

**17**

Make a tight coil using a light yellow strip (see page 11). Cover it using a bubblegum pink strip (see page 11). Apply a thin layer of glue to the bottom of the coil. Place it below the steps 10 and 16 coils.

**18**

Make a smaller open coil using a purple strip. Apply a thin layer of glue to the bottom of the coil and place it above the step 16 coil, with the end of the strip curving down from right to left.

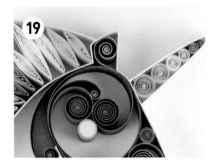

**19**

Make an open coil using a bubblegum pink strip. Apply a thin layer of glue to the bottom of the coil and place it in the ear, with the end of the strip curving from left down to the right.

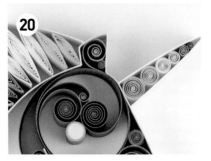

**20**

Make a very small coil using a teal strip. Apply a thin layer of glue to the bottom of the coil and place it in the bottom right of the ear.

**21**

Make an asymmetric scroll using a mint strip (see page 12). Apply a thin layer of glue to the bottom of the scroll. Place it in the horse's neck, with the end of the strip curving up from the bottom right.

**22**

Make an open coil using a light green strip. Apply a thin layer of glue to the bottom of the coil and place it above the step 21 coil, with the end of the strip curving up from the bottom left.

**23**

Make a smaller open coil using a light blue strip. Apply a thin layer of glue to the bottom of the coil and place it above the step 22 coil, with the end of the strip curving up from the bottom left.

**24**

Make a tight coil using a cream strip. Apply a thin layer of glue to the bottom of the coil and place it to the right of the step 21 and 22 coils.

**25**

Make a coil using a blue strip. Apply a thin layer of glue to the bottom of the coil and place to the right of the step 21 and 22 coils.

**26**

Make an S scroll, adapting the shape as shown here, using a bubblegum pink strip (see page 12).

**27**

Apply a thin layer of glue to the bottom of the shape. Place it above the unicorn's legs, with the strip curving from above left and around the big coil, ending with the small coil on the bottom right.

**28**

Make a coil using a yellow strip. Apply a thin layer of glue to the bottom of the coil and place it inside the circle formed by the shape in step 27, to the right of its coil.

**29**

Make an open coil using a light pink strip. Apply a thin layer of glue to the bottom of the coil. Place it in the top right of the step 27 circle, with the end of the strip curving from above to the left.

**30**

Make a tight coil using a cream strip and cover it using a purple strip. Apply a thin layer of glue to the bottom of the coil and place it to the left of the step 28 yellow coil.

**31**

Make a smaller coil using an amber strip. Apply a thin layer of glue to the bottom of the coil and place it to the left of the coil applied in step 30.

**32**

Make a coil using a purple strip and cover it using a cream strip. Apply a thin layer of glue to the bottom of the coil and place it on the left, between the steps 21 and 27 shapes.

**33**

Make a coil using a lilac strip. Apply a thin layer of glue to the bottom of the coil and place it on the right, between the steps 21 and 27 shapes.

**34**

Make an open coil using a lavender strip. Apply a thin layer of glue to the bottom of the coil and place it above the small coil of the step 27 S scroll, with the end of the strip curving upwards from the bottom right.

**35**

Make a marquise shape using a blue strip. Cover it using a cream strip. Apply a thin layer of glue to the bottom of the shape and place it at the top left corner of the right leg.

**36**

Make a smaller marquise shape using a blue strip. Apply a thin layer of glue to the bottom of the shape and place it to the right of the marquise shape applied in step 35.

**37**

Make a smaller marquise shape using a teal strip. Apply a thin layer of glue to the bottom of the shape and place it to the right of the previous marquise.

**38**

Make a smaller marquise shape using a mint strip. Apply a thin layer of glue to the bottom of the shape and place it to the right of the previous marquise.

**39**

Make an open coil using a light blue strip. Apply a thin layer of glue to the bottom of the open coil and place it as shown, with the end of the strip curving from above, then under the marquises.

**40**

Make an open coil using a lilac strip. Apply a thin layer of glue to the bottom of the coil and place it under the previous strip, with the coil on the right and the end of the strip curving down from right to left.

**41**

Make a coil using a lavender strip. Apply a thin layer of glue to the bottom of the coil and place it in the bottom left of the right leg, with the end of the strip curving from below right up the left side.

**42**

Make an S scroll using a light green strip. Apply a thin layer of glue to the bottom of the scroll. Place it to the right of the step 39 coil, with the end of the strip curving from below left of the big coil to above the small coil.

**43**

Make an open coil using a bubblegum pink strip. Apply a thin layer of glue to the bottom of the coil and place it to the right of the scroll applied in step 42.

**44**

Make a marquise shape using an amber strip. Apply a thin layer of glue to the bottom of the shape and place it in the bottom of the right hoof.

**45**

Make a marquise shape using a yellow strip. Apply a thin layer of glue to the bottom of the shape and place it in the right hoof, above the previous marquise.

Make a marquise shape using a light yellow strip. Apply a thin layer of glue to the bottom of the shape and place it above the marquise applied in step 45.

Make a coil using a purple strip. Apply a thin layer of glue to the bottom of the coil and place it on the right-hand side of the hoof, between the bottom two marquises.

Make another coil using a bubblegum pink strip. Apply a thin layer of glue to the bottom of the coil and place it on the right-hand side of the hoof, between the top two marquises.

Make an asymmetric scroll using a violet strip. Apply a thin layer of glue to the bottom of the scroll. Place it in the right leg, with the coil above the hoof and the end of the strip curving from below left up to the knee.

Make an open coil using a purple strip. Apply a thin layer of glue to the bottom of the coil and place it to the left of the step 49 coil and above the strip, with the end of the strip curving up from right to left.

Make an open coil using a teal strip. Apply a thin layer of glue to the bottom of the coil and place it below the step 49 strip, with the end of the strip curving from above left of the coil down to the right.

Make a smaller open coil using a blue strip. Apply a thin layer of glue to the bottom of the coil and place it below the step 51 strip, with the end of the strip curving from above left down to the right.

Make another smaller open coil using a light pink strip. Apply a thin layer of glue to the bottom of the coil. Place it inside the step 43 coil, with the end of the strip curving down from the left and up the right side.

Make a smaller coil using a yellow strip. Apply a thin layer of glue to the bottom of the coil and place it above the coil applied in step 53.

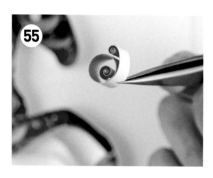

Make a C scroll, adapting the shape as shown here, using a mint strip (see page 12).

Apply a thin layer of glue to the bottom of the shape and place it in the bottom of the left hoof.

Make an open coil using a light blue strip. Apply a thin layer of glue to the bottom of the coil. Place it inside the step 55 scroll, with the end of the strip curving down from the left and up the right side.

Make an open coil using a violet strip. Apply a thin layer of glue to the bottom of the coil and place it in the top part of the left leg, with the end of the strip curving from above right to left.

Make an asymmetric scroll using a lavender strip. Apply a thin layer of glue to the bottom of the scroll. Place it above the left hoof, with the end of the strip curving from bottom left up to the right.

Make an open coil using a bubblegum pink strip. Apply a thin layer of glue to the bottom of the coil and place it to the left of the step 59 scroll, above the strip, with the end of the strip curving up from the bottom right.

Make a smaller coil using a yellow strip. Apply a thin layer of glue to the bottom of the coil and place it above the step 59 scroll.

Make a tight coil using a cream strip and cover it using a teal strip. Apply a thin layer of glue to the bottom of the coil and place it below right of the step 58 coil.

Make a smaller coil using a blue strip. Apply a thin layer of glue to the bottom of the coil and place it to the right of the step 62 coil.

64

Make an open coil using a purple strip. Apply a thin layer of glue to the bottom of the coil and place it in the bottom left corner of the left leg, with the end of the strip curving from above right to left.

65

Make a smaller open coil using a blue strip. Apply a thin layer of glue to the bottom of the coil and place it in the bottom right corner of the left hoof, with the end of the strip curving from right.

# Templates

All the templates are shown at actual size
and can be traced or photocopied and cut out.

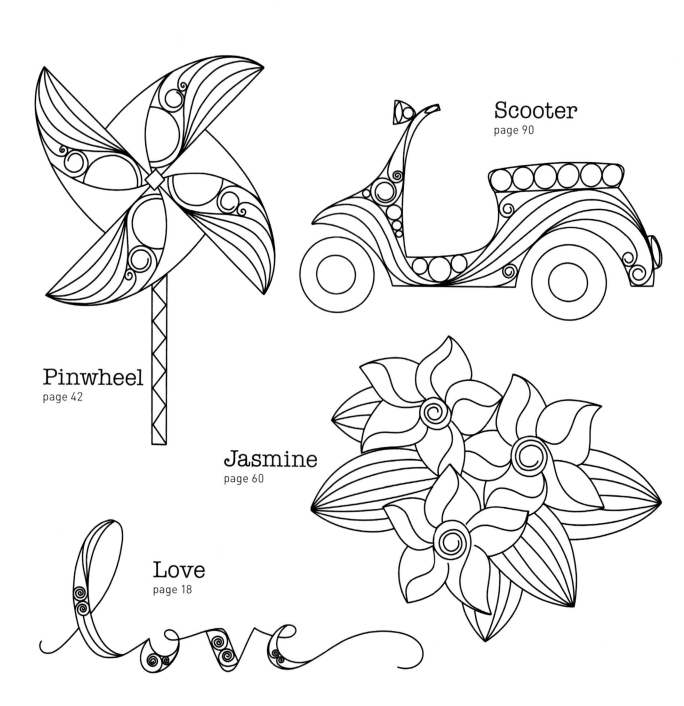

**Scooter**
page 90

**Pinwheel**
page 42

**Jasmine**
page 60

**Love**
page 18

Picnic basket
page 54

Swan
page 66

Ice cream
page 48

Cheesecake
page 36

Unicorn
page 136

Mandala
page 114

Aeroplane
page 84

Tree
page 30

**Cupcake**
page 78

**Bird**
page 96

**Rainbow**
page 24

**Ampersand**
page 102

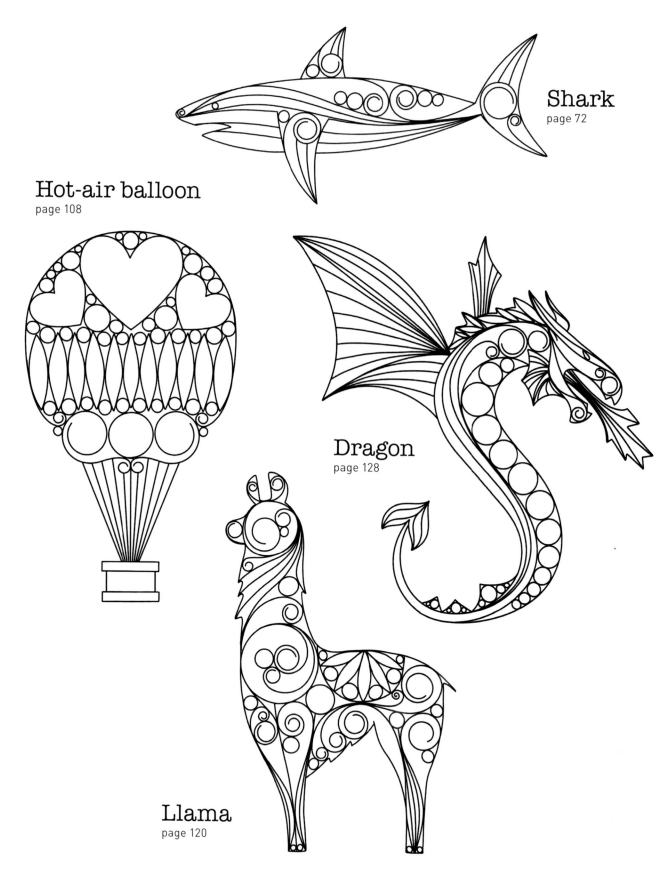

**Shark**
page 72

**Hot-air balloon**
page 108

**Dragon**
page 128

**Llama**
page 120

# Index

First published 2020 by
Guild of Master Craftsman Publications Ltd
Castle Place, 166 High Street, Lewes,
East Sussex, BN7 1XU, UK

ISBN 978 1 78494 561 9

A catalogue record for this book is available
from the British Library.

Publisher  Jonathan Bailey
Production  Jim Bulley, Jo Pallett
Senior Project Editor  Dominique Page
Editor  Theresa Bebbington
Managing Art Editor  Gilda Pacitti
Art Editor  Rebecca Mothersole
Photographers  Andrew Perris, Sena Runa

Colour origination by GMC Reprographics
Printed and bound in Malaysia

To order a book, or to request a catalogue, contact: GMC Publications Ltd,  Castle Place, 166 High Street, Lewes, East Sussex,
BN7 1XU, United Kingdom Tel: +44 (0)1273 488005

www.gmcbooks.com